Bloom's BioCritiques

DANTE ALIGHIERI

Edited and with an introduction by
Harold Bloom
Sterling Professor of the Humanities
Yale University

D0075396

CHELSEA HOUSE
PUBLISHERS
A Haights Cross Communications Company
Philadelphia

©2003 by Chelsea House Publishers, a subsidiary of
Haights Cross Communications.

A Haights Cross Communications ⬥✈ Company

Introduction © 2003 by Harold Bloom.

All rights reserved. No part of this publication may be
reproduced or transmitted in any form or by any means
without the written permission of the publisher.

Printed and bound in the United States of America

10 9 8 7 6 5 4 3 2 1

Library of Congress Cataloging-in-Publication Data

Dante Alighieri / edited and with an introduction by Harold Bloom.
     p. cm. — (Bloom's Biocritiques)
Includes bibliographical references and index.
  ISBN 0-7910-6366-6
  1. Dante Alighieri, 1265-1321. 2. Authors, Italian—To
1500—Biography. I. Bloom, Harold. II. Series.
PQ4335 .D28 2002
851'.1—dc21

2002010267

851.1
DANTE

Chelsea House Publishers
1974 Sproul Road, Suite 400
Broomall, PA 19008-0914

http://www.chelseahouse.com

Contributing editor:. Elizabeth A. S. Beaudin

Cover image: Hulton/ Archive by Getty Images

Cover design by Keith Trego

Layout by EJB Publishing Services

Centerville Library
Washington-Centerville Public Library
Centerville, Ohio

DISCARD

Bloom's BioCritiques

CONTENTS

USER'S GUIDE

These volumes are designed to introduce the reader to the life and work of the world's literary masters. Each volume begins with Harold Bloom's essay "The Work in the Writer" and a volume-specific introduction also written by Professor Bloom. Following these unique introductions is an engaging biography that discusses the major life events and important literary accomplishments of the author under consideration.

Furthermore, each volume includes an original critique that not only traces the themes, symbols, and ideas apparent in the author's works, but strives to put those works into a cultural and historical perspective. In addition to the original critique is a brief selection of significant critical essays previously published on the author and his or her works followed by a concise and informative chronology of the writer's life. Finally, each volume concludes with a bibliography of the writer's works, a list of additional readings, and an index of important themes and ideas.

HAROLD BLOOM

The Work in the Writer

Literary biography found its masterpiece in James Boswell's *Life of Samuel Johnson*. Boswell, when he treated Johnson's writings, implicitly commented upon Johnson as found in his work, even as in the great critic's life. Modern instances of literary biography, such as Richard Ellmann's lives of W. B. Yeats, James Joyce, and Oscar Wilde, essentially follow in Boswell's pattern.

That the writer somehow is in the work, we need not doubt, though with William Shakespeare, writer-of-writers, we almost always need to rely upon pure surmise. The exquisite rancidities of the Problem Plays or Dark Comedies seem to express an extraordinary estrangement of Shakespeare from himself. When we read or attend *Troilus and Cressida* and *Measure for Measure*, we may be startled by particular speeches of Ulysses in the first play, or of Vincentio in the second. These speeches, of Ulysses upon hierarchy or upon time, or of Duke Vincentio upon death, are too strong either for their contexts or for the characters of their speakers. The same phenomenon occurs with Parolles, the military impostor of *All's Well That Ends Well*. Utterly disgraced, he nevertheless affirms: "Simply the thing I am/Shall make me live."

In Shakespeare, more even than in his peers, Dante and Cervantes, meaning always starts itself again through excess or overflow. The strongest of Shakespeare's creatures—Falstaff, Hamlet, Iago, Lear, Cleopatra—have an exuberance that is fiercer than their plays can contain. If Ben Jonson was at all correct in his complaint that "Shakespeare wanted art," it could have been only in a sense that he may not have intended. Where do the personalities of Falstaff or Hamlet touch a limit? What was it in Shakespeare that made the two parts of *Henry IV* and *Hamlet* into "plays unlimited"? Neither Falstaff nor Hamlet will be stopped: their wit, their beautiful, laughing speech, their intensity of being—all these are virtually infinite.

In what ways do Falstaff and Hamlet manifest the writer in the work? Evidently, we can never know, or know enough to answer with any authority. But what would happen if we reversed the question, and asked: How did the work form the writer, Shakespeare?

Of Shakespeare's inwardness, his biography tells us nothing. And yet, to an astonishing extent, Shakespeare created our inwardness. At the least, we can speculate that Shakespeare so lived his life as to conceal the depths of his nature, particularly as he rather prematurely aged. We do not have Shakespeare on Shakespeare, as any good reader of the Sonnets comes to realize: they do not constitute a key that unlocks his heart. No sequence of sonnets could be less confessional or more powerfully detached from the poet's self.

The German poet and universal genius, Goethe, affords a superb contrast to Shakespeare. Of Goethe's life, we know more than everything; I wonder sometimes if we know as much about Napoleon or Freud or any other human being who ever has lived, as we know about Goethe. Everywhere, we can find Goethe in his work, so much so that Goethe seems to crowd the writing out, just as Byron and Oscar Wilde seem to usurp their own literary accomplishments. Goethe, cunning beyond measure, nevertheless invested a rival exuberance in his greatest works that could match his personal charisma. The sublime outrageousness of the Second Part of *Faust*, or of the greater lyric and meditative poems, form a Counter-Sublime to Goethe's own daemonic intensity.

Goethe was fascinated by the daemonic in himself; we can doubt that Shakespeare had any such interests. Evidently, Shakespeare abandoned his acting career just before he composed *Measure for Measure* and *Othello*. I surmise that the egregious interventions by Vincentio and Iago displace the actor's energies into a new kind of mischief-making, a fresh opening to a subtler playwriting-within-the-play.

But what had opened Shakespeare to this new awareness? The answer is the work in the writer, *Hamlet* in Shakespeare. One can go further: it was not so much the play, *Hamlet*, as the character Hamlet, who changed Shakespeare's art forever.

Hamlet's personality is so large and varied that it rivals Goethe's own. Ironically Goethe's Faust, his Hamlet, has no personality at all, and is as colorless as Shakespeare himself seems to have chosen to be. Yet nothing could be more colorful than the Second Part of *Faust*, which is peopled by an astonishing array of monsters, grotesque devils, and classical ghosts.

A contrast between Shakespeare and Goethe demonstrates that in each—but in very different ways—we can better find the work in the person, than we can discover that banal entity, the person in the work. Goethe to many of his contemporaries, seemed to be a mortal god. Shakespeare, so far as we know, seemed an affable, rather ordinary fellow, who aged early and became somewhat withdrawn. Yet Faust, though Mephistopheles battles for his soul, is hardly worth the trouble unless you take him as an idea and not as a person. Hamlet is nearly every-idea-in-one, but he is precisely a personality and a person.

Would Hamlet be so astonishingly persuasive if his father's ghost did not haunt him? Falstaff is more alive than Prince Hal, who says that the devil haunts him in the shape of an old fat man. Three years before composing the final *Hamlet*, Shakespeare invented Falstaff, who then never ceased to haunt his creator. Falstaff and Hamlet may be said to best represent the work in the writer, because their influence upon Shakespeare was prodigious. W.H. Auden accurately observed that Falstaff possesses infinite energy: never tired, never bored, and absolutely both witty and happy until Hal's rejection destroys him. Hamlet too has infinite energy, but in him it is more curse than blessing.

Falstaff and Hamlet can be said to occupy the roles in Shakespeare's invented world that Sancho Panza and Don Quixote possess in Cervantes's. Shakespeare's plays from 1610 on (starting with *Twelfth Night*) are thus analogous to the Second Part of Cervantes's epic novel. Sancho and the Don overtly jostle Cervantes for authorship in the Second Part, even as Cervantes battles against the impostor who has pirated a continuation of his work. As a dramatist, Shakespeare manifests the work in the writer more indirectly. Falstaff's prose genius is revived in the scapegoating of Malvolio by Maria and Sir Toby Belch, while Falstaff's darker insights are developed by Feste's melancholic wit. Hamlet's intellectual resourcefulness, already deadly, becomes poisonous in Iago and in Edmund. Yet we have not crossed into the deeper abysses of the work in the writer in later Shakespeare.

No fictive character, before or since, is Falstaff's equal in self-trust. Sir John, whose delight in himself is contagious, has total confidence both in his self-awareness and in the resources of his language. Hamlet, whose self is as strong, and whose language is as copious, nevertheless distrusts both the self and language. Later Shakespeare is, as it were, much under the influence both of Falstaff and of Hamlet, but they tug him in opposite directions. Shakespeare's own copiousness of language is well-nigh incredible: a vocabulary in excess of twenty-one thousand words, almost eighteen hundred of which he coined himself. And of his word-hoard, nearly half are used only once each, as though the perfect setting for each had been found, and need not be repeated. Love for language and faith in language are Falstaffian attributes. Hamlet will darken both that love and that faith in Shakespeare, and perhaps the Sonnets can best be read as Falstaff and Hamlet counterpointing against one another.

Can we surmise how aware Shakespeare was of Falstaff and Hamlet, once they had played themselves into existence? *Henry IV, Part I* appeared in six quarto editions during Shakespeare's lifetime; *Hamlet* possibly had four. Falstaff and Hamlet were played again and again at the Globe, but Shakespeare knew also that they were being read, and he must have had contact with some of those readers. What would it have been like to discuss Falstaff or Hamlet with one of their early readers (presumably also part of their audience at the Globe), if you were the creator of such demiurges? The question would seem nonsensical to most Shakespeare scholars, but then these days they tend to be either ideologues or moldy figs. How can we recover the uncanniness of Falstaff and of Hamlet, when they now have become so familiar?

A writer's influence upon himself is an unexplored problem in criticism, but such an influence is never free from anxieties. The biocritical problem (which this series attempts to explore) can be divided into two areas, difficult to disengage fully. Accomplished works affect the author's life, and also affect her subsequent writings. It is simpler for me to surmise the effect of *Mrs. Dalloway* and *To the Lighthouse* upon Woolf's late *Between the Acts*, than it is to relate Clarissa Dalloway's suicide and Lily Briscoe's capable endurance in art to the tragic death and complex life of Virginia Woolf.

There are writers whose lives were so vivid that they seem sometimes to obscure the literary achievement: Byron, Wilde, Malraux, Hemingway. But most major Western writers do not live that exuberantly, and the greatest of all, Shakespeare, sometimes appears to have adopted the personal mask of colorlessness. And yet there are heroes of literature who struggled titanically with their own eras—Tolstoy, Milton, Victor Hugo—who nevertheless matter more for their works than their lives.

There are great figures—Emily Dickinson, Wallace Stevens, Willa Cather—who seem to have had so little of the full intensity of life when compared to the vitality of their work, that we might almost speak of the work in the work, rather than even of the work in a person. Emily Brontë might well be the extreme instance of such a visionary, surpassing William Blake in that one regard.

I conclude this general introduction to a series of literary bio-critiques by stating a tentative formula or principle for gauging the many ways in which the work influences the person and her subsequent, later work. Our influence upon ourselves is always related to the Shakespearean invention of self-overhearing, which I have written about in several other contexts. Life, as well as poetry and prose, is overheard rather than simply heard. The writer listens to herself as though she were somebody else, and the will to change begins to operate. The forces that live in us include the prior work we have done, and the dreams and waking visions that evade our dismissals.

HAROLD BLOOM

Introduction

I

Dante, by common consent, stands with the supreme Western masters of literary representation: the Yahwist, Homer, Chaucer, Shakespeare, Cervantes, Milton, Tolstoi, Proust. Our ideas as to how reality can be represented by literary language depend, to a considerable extent, on this ninefold. Perhaps it can also be said that these writers have formed a large part of our experience of what is called reality. Certain aspects of reality might not be nearly so visible, had we not read these nine masters of mimesis. Setting the Yahwist and Homer aside as being both ancient and hypothetical, only Shakespeare, again by common consent, is judged to be Dante's rival as a great Original in representation. But Shakespearean representation has naturalized us in its domain. Dante is now an immensely difficult poet partly because we are so much at home with Shakespeare.

Erich Auerbach, who with Charles S. Singleton and John Freccero makes up a celestial trinity of Dante interpreters, gave us the definitive opening description of Dante's ways of representing reality:

> ... Dante in the *Comedy* transcended tragic death by identifying man's ultimate fate with the earthly unity of his

personality, and ... the very plan of the work made it possible, and indeed confronted him with the obligation, to represent earthly reality exactly as he saw it. Thus it became necessary that the characters in Dante's other world, in their situation and attitude, should represent the sum of themselves; that they should disclose, in a single act, the character and fate that had filled out their lives ...

... from classical theory Dante took over only one principle, the *sibi constare*, or consistency, of his persons; all other tenets had lost their literal meaning for him ... Dante's vision is a tragedy according to Aristotle's definition. In any event it is far more a tragedy than an epic, for the descriptive, epic elements in the poem are not autonomous, but serve other purposes, and the time, for Dante as well as his characters, is not the epic time in which destiny gradually unfolds, but the final time in which it is fulfilled.

If time is the final time, past all unfolding, then reality indeed can be represented in a single act that is at once character and fate. Dante's personages can reveal themselves totally in what they say and do, but they cannot change *because* of what Dante has them say and do. Chaucer, who owed Dante more than he would acknowledge, nevertheless departed from Dante in this, which is precisely where Chaucer most influenced Shakespeare. The Pardoner listens to himself speaking, listens to his own tale, and is darkly made doom-eager through just that listening. This mode of representation expands in Shakespeare to a point that no writer since has reached so consistently. Hamlet may be the most metamorphic of Shakespeare's people (or it may be Cleopatra, or Falstaff, or who you will), but as such he merely sets the mode. Nearly everyone of consequence in Shakespeare helps inaugurate a mimetic style we all now take too much for granted. They, like us, are strengthened or victimized, reach an apotheosis or are destroyed, by themselves reacting to what they say and do. It may be that we have learned to affect ourselves so strongly, in part because involuntarily we imitate Shakespeare's characters. We never imitate Dante's creatures because we do not live in finalities; we know that we are not fulfilled.

A literary text can represent a fulfilled reality only if it can persuade itself, and momentarily persuade us, that one text can fulfill another. Dante, as Auerbach demonstrated, relied upon the great Christian trope of *figura*, whose basis was the insistence that the Christian New Testament had fulfilled what it called "the Old Testament," itself a phrase deeply offensive to normative Jews who continue to trust in the Covenant as set forth in the Hebrew Bible. But the Hebrew Bible indeed must be the Old Testament, if Christianity is to retain its power. What must the New Testament be, if Dante's poem is to develop and maintain its force?

Auerbach, quoting the Church Father Tertullian's comments upon the renaming of Oshea, son of Nun, by Moses as Jehoshua (Joshua, Jesus), speaks of Joshua as "a figure of things to come." The definition of this figure of prophecy or *figura* by Auerbach is now classic: "*Figura* is something real and historical which announces something else that is real and historical." Equally classic is Auerbach's formulation of "figural interpretation":

> Figural interpretation establishes a connection between two events or persons, the first of which signifies not only itself but also the second, while the second encompasses or fulfills the first. The first two poles of the figure are separate in time, but both, being real events or figures, are within time, within the stream of historical life. Only the understanding of the two persons or events is a spiritual act, but this spiritual act deals with concrete events whether past, present, or future, and not with concepts or abstractions; these are quite secondary, since promise and fulfillment are real historical events, which have either happened in the incarnation of the word, or will happen in the second coming.

What happens when figural interpretation is transferred from sacred to secular literature? When Dante takes the historical Virgil and reads him as a *figura* of which Dante's character, Virgil, is the fulfillment, are we seeing the same pattern enacted as when Tertullian reads Joshua as the *figura* of which Jesus Christ was the fulfillment? Auerbach's answer is "yes," but this is a dialectical affirmative: "Thus Virgil in the *Divine Comedy* is the historical Virgil himself, but then again he is not; for the historical Virgil is only a *figura* of the fulfilled truth that the poem reveals, and this fulfillment is more real, more significant than the *figura*." Auerbach, writing on *figura* back in 1944, thought back to his book on Dante as poet of the secular world (1929), from which I quoted earlier, and insisted that he had acquired "a solid historical grounding" for his view of fifteen years before.

I am not certain that the earlier Auerbach is not to be preferred to the later. In securalizing *figura*, Auerbach dangerously idealized the relationship between literary texts. Appropriating the historical, Virgil is not an idealizing gesture, as John Freccero shows in his superb essay, "Manfred's Wounds and the Poetics of the *Purgatorio*." Poetic fathers die hard, and Dante understood that he had made the historical Virgil the *figura*, and his own Virgil the fulfillment, partly in order to suggest that he himself was the poet Virgil's true fulfillment. Great poets are pragmatists when they deal with precursors; witness Blake's caricature of Milton as the hero of his poem *Milton*, or James Merrill's loving and witty portrayal of Stevens and Auden in *The Changing Light at Sandover*. Dante's Virgil is no more the historical Virgil than Blake's Milton is the historical Milton. If texts fulfill one another, it is always through some self-serving caricature of the earlier text by the later.

II

Charles S. Singleton, carefully reminding us that "Beatrice is not Christ," expounds Dante's use of the principle of analogy which likens the advent of Beatrice to the advent of Christ:

> Thus it is that the figure of a rising sun by which Beatrice comes at last to stand upon the triumphal chariot is the most revealing image which the poet might have found not only to affirm the analogy of her advent to Christ's in the present tense, but to stress, in so doing, the very basis upon which that analogy rests: the advent of light.

Whitman, certainly a poet antithetical to Dante, opposed himself to the rising sun as a greater rising sun:

> Dazzling and tremendous how quick the sun-rise would kill me,
> > If I could not now and always send sun-rise out of me.

We also ascend dazzling and tremendous as the sun,
We found our own O my soul in the calm and cool of
the daybreak.

This is not analogy but a subversive mode akin to Nietzsche's, and learned from Emerson. The figure of the Whitmanian sun here is not an advent of Christ ("a great defeat" Emerson called that advent) but is "now and always," a perpetual dawning ("we demand victory," as Emerson said for his Americans, prophesying Whitman). The figure of Beatrice, to Whitman, might as well have been the figure of Christ. Can we, with Singleton, accept her as an analogy, or is she now the principal embarrassment of Dante's poem? As a fiction she retains her force, but does not Dante present her as more than a fiction? If Dante wrote, as Singleton says, the allegory of the theologians rather than the allegory of the poets, how are we to recapture Dante's sense of Beatrice if we do not accept the analogy that likens her advent to Christ's?

Singleton's answer is that Beatrice is the representation of Wisdom in a Christian sense, or the light of Grace. This answer, though given in the allegorical language of the theologians rather than that of the poets, remains a poetic answer because its analogical matrix is light rather than Grace. Dante persuades us not by his theology but by his occult mastery of the trope of light, in which he surpasses even the blind Milton among the poets:

There is a light up there which makes the Creator visible to
the creature, who finds his peace only in seeing Him.
(*Paradiso* XXX, 100–102)

This, as Singleton says, is the Light of Glory rather than the Light of Grace, which is Beatrice's, or the Natural Light, which is Virgil's. Dante's peculiar gift is to find perpetually valid analogies for all three lights. Since his poem's fiction of duration is not temporal, but final, all three modes of light must be portrayed by him as though they were beyond change. And yet an unchanging fiction cannot give pleasure, as Dante clearly knew. What does he give us that more than compensates for his poem's apparent refusal of temporal anguish?

Auerbach, in his essay on St. Francis of Assisi in the *Commedia*, turned to *figura* again as his answer. To the medieval reader, according to Auerbach, the representations of forerunning and after-following repetitions were as familiar as the trope of "historical development" is (or was, to those who believe that Foucault forever exposed the trope). To us, now, "forerunning and after-following repetitions" suggest, not *figura* and its fulfillment, but the Freudian death-drive as the "fulfillment" of the compulsion-to-repeat. The repetition-compulsion perhaps is the final Western *figura*, prophesying our urge to drive beyond the pleasure principle. That is to say, for us the only text that can fulfill earlier texts, rather than correct or negate them, is what might be called "the text of death," which is totally opposed to what Dante sought to write.

III

What saves Dante from the idealizing lameness that necessarily haunts the allegorizing of the theologians? The earlier Auerbach was on the track of the answer when he meditated upon Dante's originality in the representation of persons. As seer, Dante identified character and fate, *ethos* and *daemon*, and what he saw in his contemporaries he transferred precisely to the three final worlds of *Inferno*, *Purgatorio*, and *Paradiso*. Dante's friends and enemies alike are presented, without ambiguity or ambivalence, as being consistent with themselves, beyond change, their eternal destinies over-determined by their fixed characters.

There are endless surprises in his poem for Dante himself, as for us, but there are no accidents. Farinata standing upright in his tomb, as if of Hell he had a great disdain, is heroic because he is massively consistent with himself, in his own tomb, can be nothing but what he is. His marvelous disdain of Hell represents a kind of necessity, what Wallace Stevens called the inescapable necessity of being that inescapable animal, oneself. Such a necessity is presented by Dante as being the judgment of Heaven upon us.

In Shakespeare, there are always accidents, and character can be as metamorphic as personality. Hamlet yields himself up to accident, at the last, perhaps because he has all but exhausted the possibilities for change that even his protean character possesses. This is our mode of representation, inherited by us from Shakespeare, and we no longer are able to see how original it originally was. Shakespeare therefore seems "natural" to us, even though we live in the age of Freud, who suspected darkly that there were no accidents, once we were past infancy. Dante no longer can be naturalized in our imaginations. His originality has not been lost for us, and yet his difficulty or strangeness for us is probably not caused by his authentic originality.

The allegory of the theologians simply is not an available mode for us, despite the labors of Auerbach and Singleton. Freccero has replaced them as the most relevant of Dante critics because he has returned Dante to what may be the truest, because least idealizing, allegory of the poets, which is the agon of poet against poet, the struggle for imaginative priority between forerunner and latecomer. Despite a marvelous parody by Borges, theologians are not primarily agonists. Dante understood that poets were. The light of glory, the light of grace, the light of nature are not competing lights, and yet all tropes for them necessarily compete, and always with other tropes.

Singleton, rejecting the allegory of the poets, said that it would reduce Dante's Virgil to a mere personification of Reason:

> For if this is the allegory of poets, then what Virgil does, like what Orpheus does, is a fiction devised to convey a hidden meaning which it ought to convey all the time, since only by conveying that other meaning is what he does justified at all. Instead, if this action is allegory as theologians take it, then this action must always have a literal sense which is historical and no fiction; and thus Virgil's deeds as part of the whole action may, in their turn, be as words signifying other things, but they do not have to do this all the time, because, being historical, those deeds exist simply in their own right.

But what if Virgil, as allegory of the poets, were to be read not as Reason, the light of nature, but as the trope of that light, reflecting among much else the lustres of the tears of universal nature? To say farewell to Virgil is to take leave not of Reason, but of the pathos of a certain natural light, perhaps of Wordsworth's "light of common day." Dante abandons Virgil not so as to substitute grace for reason, but so as to find his own image of voice, his own trope for all three lights. In the oldest and most authentic allegory of the poets, Virgil represents not reason but poetic fatherhood, the Scene of Instruction that Dante must transcend if he is to complete his journey to Beatrice.

IV

The figure of Beatrice, in my own experience as a reader, is now the most difficult of all Dante's tropes, because sublimation no longer seems to be a human possibility. What is lost, perhaps permanently, is the tradition that moves between Dante and Yeats, in which sublimated desire for a woman can be regarded as an enlargement of existence. One respected feminist critic has gone so far as to call Beatrice a "dumb broad," since she supposedly contemplates the One without understanding Him. What James Thurber grimly celebrated as the War between Men and Women has claimed many recent literary casualties, but none perhaps so unmerited as Dante's Beatrice. Dante, like tradition, thought that God's Wisdom, who daily played before His feet, was a woman, even as Nietzsche, with a gesture beyond irony, considered Truth to be a woman, presumably a deathly one. We possess art in order not to perish from the truth, Nietzsche insisted, which must mean that the aesthetic is a way of not being destroyed by a woman. Dante hardly would have agreed.

Beatrice is now so difficult to apprehend precisely because she participates both in the allegory of the poets and in the allegory of the philosophers. Her advent follows Dante's poetic maturation, or the vanishing of the precursor, Virgil. In the allegory of the poets, Beatrice is the Muse, whose function is to help the poet remember. Since remembering, in poetry, is the major mode of cognition, Beatrice is Dante's power of invention, the essence of his art. That means she is somehow the highest of the Muses, and yet far above them also, since in Dante's version of the allegory of the poets, Beatrice has "a place in the objective process of salvation," as Ernst Robert Curtius phrased it. Curtius rightly emphasized the extent of Dante's audacity:

> Guido Guinicelli (d. 1276) had made the exaltation of the beloved to an angel of paradise a topos of Italian lyric. To choose as guide in a poetic vision of the otherworld a loved woman who has been thus exalted is still within the bounds of Christian philosophy and faith. But Dante goes much further than this. He gives Beatrice a place in the objective process of salvation. Her function is thought of as not only for himself but also for all believers. Thus, on his own

authority, he introduces into the Christian revelation an element which disrupts the doctrine of the church. This is either heresy—or myth.

It is now customary to speak of Dante as *the* Catholic poet, even as Milton is called *the* Protestant poet. Perhaps someday Kafka will be named as *the* Jewish writer, though his distance from normative Judaism was infinite. Dante and Milton were not less idiosyncratic, each in his own time, than Kafka was in ours, and the figure of Beatrice would be heresy and not myth if Dante had not been so strong a poet that the Church of later centuries has been happy to claim him. Curtius centered upon Dante's vision of himself as a prophet, even insisting that Dante expected the prophecy's fulfillment in the immediate future, during his own lifetime. Since Dante died at the age of fifty-six, a quarter-century away from the "perfect" age of eighty-one set forth in his *Convivio*, the literal force of the prophecy presumably was voided. But the prophecy, still hidden from us, matters nevertheless, as Curtius again maintains:

Even if we could interpret his prophecy, that would give it no meaning for us. What Dante hid, Dante scholarship need not now unriddle. But it must take seriously the fact that Dante believed that he had an apocalyptic mission. This must be taken into consideration in interpreting him. Hence the question of Beatrice is not mere idle curiosity. Dante's system is built up in the first two cantos of the *Inferno*, it supports the entire *Commedia*. Beatrice can be seen only within it. The Lady Nine has become a cosmic power which emanates from two superior powers. A hierarchy of celestial powers which intervene in the process of history—this concept is manifestly related to Gnosticism: as an intellectual construction, a schema of intellectual contemplation, if perhaps not in origin. Such constructions can and must be pointed out. We do not know what Dante meant by Lucia. The only proper procedure for the commentator, then, is to admit that we do not know and to say that neither the ophthalmological explanation nor the allegorical inter-pretations are satisfactory. Exegesis is also bound to give its full weight to all the passages at the end of the *Purgatorio* and in the *Paradiso* which are opposed to the identification of

Beatrice with the daughter of the banker Portinari. Beatrice
is a myth created by Dante.

Very little significant criticism of Dante has followed this
suggestion of Curtius, and a distorted emphasis upon Dante's supposed
orthodoxy has been the result. Curtius certainly does not mean that
Dante was a Gnostic, but he does remind us that Dante's Beatrice is the
central figure in a purely personal gnosis. Dante indeed was a ruthless
visionary, passionate and willful, whose poem triumphantly expresses his
own unique personality. The *Commedia*, though one would hardly know
this from most of its critics (Freccero is the sublime exception), is an
immense trope of pathos or power, the power of the individual who was
Dante. The pathos of that personality is most felt, perhaps, in the great
and final parting of Beatrice from her poet, in the middle of Canto XXXI
of the *Paradiso*, at the moment when her place as guide is transferred to
the aged St. Bernard:

> Already my glance had taken in the whole general form of
> Paradise but had not yet dwelt on any part of it, and I turned
> with new-kindled eagerness to question my Lady of things
> on which my mind was in suspense. One thing I intended,
> and another encountered me: I thought to see Beatrice, and
> I saw an old man, clothed like that glorious company. His
> eyes and his cheeks were suffused with a gracious gladness,
> and his aspect was of such kindness as befits a tender father.
> And "Where is she?" I said in haste; and he replied: "To end
> thy longing Beatrice sent me from my place; and if thou took
> up into the third circle from the highest tier thou shalt see
> her again, in the throne her merits have assigned to her."
> Without answering, I lifted up my eyes and saw her where
> she made for herself a crown, reflecting from her the eternal
> beams. From the highest region where it thunders no mortal
> eye is so far, were it lost in the depth of the sea, as was my
> sight there from Beatrice; but to me it made no difference,
> for her image came down to me undimmed by aught
> between.
> "O Lady in whom my hope has its strength and who didst
> bear for my salvation to leave thy footprints in Hell, of all the
> things that I have seen I acknowledge the grace and the

virtue to be from thy power and from thy goodness. It is thou who hast drawn me from bondage into liberty by all those ways, by every means for it that was in thy power. Preserve in me thy great bounty, so that my spirit, which thou hast made whole, may be loosed from the body well-pleasing to thee." I prayed thus; and she, so far off as she seemed, smiled and looked at me, then turned again to the eternal fount.

It is difficult to comment upon the remorseless strength of this, upon its apparent sublimation of a mythmaking drive that here accepts a restraint which is more than rhetorical. Freud in his own great *summa*, the essay of 1937, "Analysis Terminable and Interminable," lamented his inability to cure those who could not accept the cure:

A man will not be subject to a father-substitute or owe him anything and he therefore refuses to accept his cure from the physician.

Dante too would not owe any man anything, not even if the man were Virgil, his poetic father. The cure had been accepted by Dante from his physician, Beatrice. In smiling and looking at him, as they part, she confirms the cure.

ELLYN SANNA

Biography of Dante Alighieri

LOVE AT FIRST SIGHT

One day in the thirteenth century, nine-year-old Dante Alighieri went with his father to a party at the home of Folco Portinari, a wealthy banker. Many other children were at the party, including Folco's eight-year-old daughter, Beatrice. After dining, the children ran off together to play, and Dante had a chance to get to know the little girl, whose nickname was Bici. She wore scarlet, and her manners were quiet and gentle.

Despite his youth, Dante fell in love with her almost immediately. He began to tremble, overwhelmed by his feelings, for he sensed that now that he had met this girl, his life would never again be as it had been before. From now on, he told himself, life would be ruled by a new love, a new source of joy. The revelation brought both excitement and fear; he sensed that his feelings might make his life harder than it might otherwise have been. Still, he wrote later, his heart commanded him: "Behold the God who is stronger than I and who in his coming will rule over me."

This was no passing fancy. From then on, wherever he went, he was always hoping to catch a glimpse of Beatrice. He lingered in places where he knew she might be and tried to arrange "accidental" meetings. He could not stop daydreaming about her; she was the most beautiful creature he had ever seen.

Nine years after their first meeting, Dante at last had a chance to speak for the first time with the girl he loved. She was walking with two older women, and this time she was dressed all in white, as beautiful as before. To Dante's great joy, she greeted him. The meeting took place at nine o'clock in the morning, and Dante was struck by the strange importance the number nine seemed to play in Beatrice's life. He became convinced that the number bore a deeper meaning. Years later, his interpretation of that meaning would deepen; for now, however, he knew only that this young woman's beauty lifted him to a greater awareness of love and God.

His feelings were undeniable, yet he kept his love secret. He could not refrain from staring at Beatrice whenever she was nearby, but he tried to convince others that he was actually interested in another young woman, one who was often sitting close to Beatrice. Hoping to disguise his true feelings, he even went so far as to address a poem to this other girl—and his efforts were so successful that gossip quickly spread about his feelings for the other young woman. Soon after, Beatrice snubbed him in the street. Dante, crushed, sent a note to Beatrice to explain the truth of the situation, but she sent no reply.

Having little to do with love, thirteenth-century marriages served primarily as business arrangements. While Folco Portinari, debatably Beatrice's father, was an important citizen of Florence, Dante's family had a far lower social standing. Thus, Dante knew that a marriage between him and Beatrice would never be possible. Eventually, she married a banker like her father, one Simone Bardi. Dante also made an advantageous marriage, with the daughter of a good family.

However, his love was not lustful or adulterous, for he wanted nothing from Beatrice but the opportunity to admire her beauty. For the rest of his life, his thoughts would continue to focus on her. In her honor, Dante would write some of the greatest works of poetry ever composed in Europe, and her influence on his life would endure until his death. Although he spoke with her hardly more than once, she continued to be the guiding force that shaped his life and his writing.

THE WORLD OF DANTE'S BIRTH

The son born in the late spring of 1265 to Alighiero di Bellincione Alighieri and his wife, Bella, was given the name Durante—perhaps after Bella's father—but the couple soon gave their son the nickname by which he would be known until his death in 1321. Dante's birth took place in his father's 46th year; Alighiero, a notary of ancient family, and Bella, possibly of noble blood had a daughter, too, a few years later. Bella died when her children were still young, and Alighiero was married again, to Lapa Cialuffi, soon afterward. Dante's stepmother eventually bore first Francesco and then Gaetana, the boy's half-brother and half-sister.

Dante was raised in a bustling Florence that functioned like a state in its own right. In fact, at the time of Dante's birth, Florence was becoming the wealthiest city in Europe. With a population of nearly 100,000 people, it was also one of the largest. The citizens of Florence possessed a wide range of industrial and technical skills, and the city's commercial connections stretched far beyond the Mediterranean world.

The major obstacle to the development of Florence in Dante's time was its endless series of civil wars. The factions at odds were the Guelphs and the Ghibellines, two important Florentine families; some biographers have claimed, plausibly, that Dante's father was of Guelph extraction and his mother of Ghibelline. The balance of power between the two families shifted constantly; as one family rose to power, it would exile supporters of the other—and then the other family would come to power and banish supporters of the first. In 1266, shortly after Dante's birth, the Guelphs won an important victory over the Ghibellines, driving them out of the city, but this did not bring an end to the bloodshed; by 1273, when Dante was about eight years old, the violence was so prevalent throughout the Florentine streets that the Church itself felt a call to intervene, and Pope Gregory IX met with Charles of Anjou in Florence. This formal reconciliation between the families did not last, though, and brawling in the streets continued daily. Perhaps fortunately, the Alghieri family was not important enough politically to be extensively affected by these violent twists and turns.

The Italian feudal system into which Dante was born differed from those of northern and western Europe in several significant ways. The Italian nobility did not live in fortified castles or manors, as they did in England and France and Germany, but instead they made the cities their manors. Cities like Florence often had many of the characteristics of a small nation. The emerging urban middle class, particularly the merchants and professional people, was actively involved in politics and government. The boundaries that separated the nobility, the middle class, and the peasantry were more fluid than they were in other parts of

Europe, and there existed a degree of social mobility. Through marriage, a person could move into a higher class with relative ease.

Dante's parents both came from respectable, even ancient, bloodlines, but the Alighieri family was neither influential nor wealthy. By the time of Dante's youth, the family owned a house in Florence and two farms at nearby Camerata and Pagnolle. Dante's grandfather and father both had been moneylenders for a time, a profession that ranked below many others in respectability, but by the mid-1260s, Dante's father had become a small-time businessman and landowner.

Aside from his meeting with Beatrice, very little is recorded about Dante's childhood. Historians know only that he lived in a literate city, most of whose inhabitants could read and write. As a young child, Dante would have attended an elementary school, where he was instructed by one of the *doctores puerorum*, laymen who taught not only reading and writing but Latin grammar as well. Next he would likely have attended an "abacus school"; these schools taught the mathematics needed for the business world. During the final stage of Dante's public schooling, he would have continued his studies in Latin and been trained in logic, rhetoric, and poetry. His studies would have afforded him a broad introduction to Ovid, Virgil, Homer, and Horace, the ancient classical poets whose works most influenced him throughout his life.

But the opportunities to learn in Dante's Florence were by no means confined to the schoolroom. The city was an international trading center, and its merchants often journeyed to other lands, returning with knowledge and languages from other countries. From these well-traveled businessmen, Dante might have learned about the literature and artistic culture of other European nations, especially France.

BEATRICE

Inarguably, the greatest influence on Dante's early life, and certainly on his poetic development, was his emotional interaction with Beatrice, or with his idea of Beatrice. We owe the bulk of the current understanding of this influence to Dante's own recollection; shortly after his beloved's death, in 1289, he assembled and published all the sonnets she had inspired him to write. More important for the instant purpose, though, is the manner in which he published the work: he decided to include with the poems themselves, commentary on the circumstances surrounding their creation. He gave to the collection the ambiguous title *Vita Nuova*, or "new life," and in his commentary he recounted the episodes of his love for Beatrice. Although this paratext, written in Dante's twenty-fifth year, must surely be compromised by problems of memory and purpose, it nevertheless provides the only primary information available on this crucial series of events and certainly merits inclusion here.

One of the episodes Dante recounts in the *Vita Nuova*—really, of his birth as a poet—is his encounter with Beatrice at the wedding party of a mutual acquaintance. Her presence surprised him, and he was sufficiently overcome to lean against a wall and struggle not to faint. He hoped no one would notice his behavior, but a nearby group of young women soon began to point at him and whisper. Dante was mortified—particularly when he realized that Beatrice was laughing with the rest. He fled the reception in tears. Almost immediately, though, he discovered a means to assuage his embarrassment: he could mold his humiliation into a sonnet. Hoping the poem would somehow find its way to Beatrice—who, he was sure, never could laugh at him if she truly understood his feelings—he wrote:

> With your companions you make fun of me,
> Not thinking, Lady, what the reason is
> I cut so strange a figure in your eyes
> When, raising mine, your loveliness I see.

Although he had spelled out his feelings, Dante recalls, as soon as he had completed the sonnet he realized that he was no closer to understanding how he could be at once so drawn to Beatrice and so overcome in her presence. A second sonnet followed, and then a third—

> ... I come to you to remedy my plight;
> But if I raise my eyes to look at you
> So vast a tremor in my heart begins
> My beating pulses put my soul to flight.

—and with these three poems Dante felt expressed. Soon, though, he found he had many more poems to write about his love for Beatrice—though, significantly, he addressed no more of them to her.

A few weeks later, at another social gathering, he reached a crisis in his life for both his writing and his developing infatuation: he met some of the same young women who had laughed at him at the wedding party. They quizzed him on his love for Beatrice, which had been obvious to all who had witnessed his behavior. "What is the point of your love for your lady," they asked him, "since you are unable to endure her presence?"

The question was compelling. Dante's overpowering, love-at-first-sight attraction to Beatrice seemed to have little foundation in the real and therefore little chance for survival once she was out of his sight. But Dante's answer to this question changed his life. He rose to the implied challenge and reached a dramatic turning point, in both his writing and his feelings for Beatrice. His love for Beatrice, he told the young women, asked nothing of her, existed independent of her; it was completely unselfish, as all his "blessedness and joy" depended simply on his praising of her beauty.

This seems to have helped Dante's infatuation to bloom at last into the obsession that informed all his later work. Beatrice came to embody all he believed about faith and the nature of reality—a living metaphor for the divine, a vessel of God, a *communication* with God—and for the rest of his life he would find serenity in contemplating her beauty and goodness. He would write only about her.

These new ideas exhilarated. He longed to express his thoughts in writing, but he was also frightened. "Reflecting deeply on this," he recalls, still in the *Vita Nuova*, "it seemed to me that I had undertaken too lofty a theme for my powers, so much so that I was afraid to enter upon it; and so I remained for several days desiring to write and afraid to begin." But Dante was too inspired to hesitate for long. He addressed his next writing to the young women with whom he had spoken, for he felt they were the people who would be most apt to understand his meaning. "A marvel she must be which God intends," he wrote of Beatrice. "She is the sum of nature's universe."

Soon after this, Dante fell seriously ill. For nine days, he suffered terrible pain, and he feared he might die. As he lay thinking about death, he realized that one day Beatrice, too, would inevitably die. The realization sent him into a fevered delirium, full of portentous nightmares—crying out his beloved's name, he frightened his young sister, who was standing by his bed, and she began to cry; the women who were caring for him gathered around him and made attempts at comfort.

When the nine days had passed, the formerly ill Dante based six stanzas of poetry—what was referred to as a *canzone*—on a vision of his delirium. The *canzone* included these lines:

> Then to reveal the mystery came Love,
> Saying to me, "Our lady come and see."
> Still in my fantasy,
> He brought me where I saw her lying dead,
> And gathered around her bed
> Women I saw who veiled her in a robe.
> With her, in truth, was such humility
> She seemed to say, "Peace has been granted me."

Perhaps these more serious thoughts inspired Dante to begin looking at Beatrice in a new and deeper way, to codify the religious connection more clearly. Shortly after his recovery, Dante tells us in the *Vita Nuova*, he looked up by chance and saw coming toward him a girl named Giovanna, whom his friend Cavalcanti was pursuing at the time. Directly behind Giovanna was Beatrice. Dante became convinced that this circumstance, this coincidence, carried an important symbolic value.

In a world where many children never reached adulthood, where few lived longer than a half-century, the challenge of making sense of life and death was a very real one. The ideologies of Dante's time described a well-ordered universe, a universe of correspondences, echoes, omens, and reflections—a world abundant with meaning in which coincidence had not much of a place. Some have suggested that this perception of meaning functioned to reassure a frightened people that life was not to be lived in vain, that existence counted; in any case, Dante's conclusion is not unusual. He believed Beatrice's very name to be no accident: Beatrice, "one who blesses."

Dante became convinced that his brief alignment of Giovanna and Beatrice echoed the relationship between John the Baptist and Christ. The name Giovanna, he reasoned, was a feminine form of the name John, and John the Baptist was said to have preceded Christ, the "True Light," the one who had prepared the "way of the Lord," just as Giovanna had come before Beatrice. Whether these ideas truly took hold at the time, or whether Dante added them to the experience years later, is unclear; they would become significant only with their much later circulation, after Beatrice's death, as part of the *Vita Nuova*.

In any case, the complexities of Dante's artistic relationship with Beatrice did not impede his parents from arranging an advantageous marriage elsewhere. On January 9, 1277, he was officially engaged to Gemma Donati, a young girl from a very prominent Florentine family. He was only 12 years old at the time, but such an age was not unusual for marriage among the wealthy of Italy, especially given that the union would take place a full eight years later. Dante and Gemma Donati had little say in the matter; their parents would have worked out an arrangement financially and socially advantageous to both families. They were married in 1285, in Dante's twenty-first year, and their relationship seems never to have grown beyond business. Dante mentions his childhood engagement in none of his later writings, and not once in any of his works does he mention Gemma Donati by name. No comparison with Beatrice can be made.

THE POETIC SCENE

In his early 20s, the newly married Dante continued to study literature and the liberal arts, and by all evidence it is at about this time, after years of fascination, that he began to produce poetry of his own. His work seems to have been not merely a pastime or a hobby for Dante, but an essential component of his perspective on both himself and the universe. His interest grew to preoccupation, and soon he was eager to find others who felt and thought as he did. There was a circle of poets in the city at the time to which Dante hoped his work would win him admittance: this was a group of young Florentine aristocrats who labeled their work the *Dolce Stil Novo* ("sweet new style") and were endeavoring to breathe new life into Italian literature. Dante was determined to join them.

In Dante's day, poetry and literature were the popular pursuits of the leisure classes. At the time, all the most prized works of literature were in Latin, the ancient language of Rome. No known poetry at all had been written in Italian until about 40 years before Dante's birth. The change had come in the mid-1220s when a group of Sicilian poets had begun to imitate the poetry of the troubadours who traveled through Europe entertaining audiences with their songs and recitations. Unlike the troubadours, whose poems were in Latin or dialects of French, the

Sicilian poets had written *only* in their own language. Their poems were similar to the troubadours' in other ways, too: both schools of poetry wrote of love almost exclusively, and between poems the content varied little if at all. In each work, the poem's speaker, the lover, expressed his humble adoration for an aloof, often aristocratic beloved; she rarely returned the lover's feelings, and yet he was nevertheless elevated above the everyday world by his eternal devotion to his indifferent mistress. This Sicilian style falls, directly or indirectly, into the tradition of courtly love.

At about the time of Dante's birth, a poet named Guittone d'Arezzo had begun a new school of Italian poetry, advocating the expansion of subject matter *beyond* love. Arezzo himself had written many poems, on a variety of subjects, and his school of poetry was still a powerful influence when Dante first began to devote his life to writing. Like the *Stil Novo* poets whose ranks he hoped to join, Dante wrote in Italian, the vernacular or common language, rather than in the more formal and academic Latin that most poets favored. The changes in language and subject matter represent an important break with the classical and courtly traditions.

Of course, no publishers existed at the time; the practice among writers was to circulate their work among their peers. The young Dante sent his poems to more experienced poets, anonymously at first, and solicited their opinions. Among the first whom Dante approached in this way was one Dante de Maiano, an Italian troubadour now considered minor. The two young men corresponded for some time, and Dante's letters show that even in his youth he was deeply interested in intellectual matters, committed to both words and ideas.

The poem that gained him entrance at last into the *Stil Novo* circle was a sonnet that described a dream in which Love, conceptualized as medieval lord, prevails upon Beatrice to eat Dante's heart. Several *Stil Novo* poets answered Dante with sonnets of their own that interpreted his dream, and Dante became a part of the circle's poetic commerce. Dante de Maiano's response to the original sonnet was crude and mocking, but another poet, Guido Cavalcanti, sent a serious reply, inaugurating a friendship that would prove important throughout Dante's life.

Guido Cavalcanti was a member of the prestigious and powerful Guelph clan. He was somber, full of doubts about God and the nature of reality, and committed to one of the militant political factions in

Florence. His family were Epicureans; they believed that life had no greater meaning beyond physical existence, and so comfort and physical pleasure were the greatest good possible.

Cavalcanti's work dealt with the nature of love, but not in the romantic sense that had interested the troubadours. Instead, Cavalcanti strove to analyze the tension between the real and the ideal, between the senses and the mind. It was because of this tension, he claimed, that all life experiences were ultimately destructive. Indeed, he was far gloomier than Dante, and Dante's religious faith was more certain. Their many discussions stimulated Dante's intellectual growth: Cavalcanti was his alter ego, the "Devil's advocate" who helped Dante to understand his own philosophy.

Although Cavalcanti was some ten years older than Dante, the two men became close friends, and Dante would later speak of him as his *primo amico*, or best friend. The two spent much of their time together discussing the nature of love and other philosophical matters, and Dante could hardly have chosen a source of wisdom better suited to his ambitions; although the *Stil Novo* poets were greatly influenced by Guittone d'Arezzo, Cavalcanti's influence was greater still. Under Cavalcanti's leadership, the *Stil Novo* worked to write "pure" Italian; they strictly eliminated from all their poems as many French and Latin words as possible. It is clear that Cavalcanti helped to shape Dante as a writer— and if we consider the difference in their ages, and imagine Dante as a starry-eyed adolescent and Cavalcanti as a mentor, a role model, even an object of artistic reverence, then Cavalcanti's influence over Dante is hardly surprising.

Dante was also deeply influenced by another, older Florentine poet—Brunetto Latini, the diplomat credited with introducing French literature to Italy. Latini was in his late 50s by the time Dante studied with him, and although Latini was no aristocrat he nevertheless exercised enormous influence in Florence. He was a poet, but he was also a businessman, a notary whose job was to handle the city's complex legal administration. In addition to this job, he had the title of "rhetorician"; this means he was skilled in writing letters according to medieval Italy's elaborate conventions. Letter-writing was a vital diplomatic skill, and at the time of his first contact with Dante, Latini was the official secretary and letter-writer to Florence's governing council—a position of no small prestige.

It seems Latini's intention as an artist was to share his learning with the other citizens of Florence. Many of the Italian poems he wrote seem designed to present knowledge in terms that would be easy to understand, and Latini also translated into the vernacular some of the great works of classical authors like Cicero. He probably was not Dante's official tutor, but the younger poet nevertheless learned a great deal from this wise and generous man. And Dante seems to have appreciated the contribution; he praises Latini movingly in the *Inferno* and mentions one of his former teacher's seminal works.

Now that Dante had been accepted into Florence's premier circle of poets, he continued to work with the sonnet form. His early efforts mainly recount romantic situations that might be found in the earlier troubadour literature. He wrote of the torments of unrequited love and the need to keep the name of one's love a secret; the anguish of misunderstandings with the beloved and the utter joy of her presence; the embarrassment of being mocked by one's lover and the evils of Death, the villain who threatens all love and beauty.

Most of these poems were lighthearted, and Dante was probably referring to actual flirtations with various young women. His love of philosophy, the academic, and ideals of love was not so ingrained, so exclusive, as to sublimate attraction utterly; indeed, he once wrote a poem enumerating the sixty most desirable women in Florence.

As he continued to grow as a poet, though, Dante found he was most inspired when he set aside the idealized romance to write about Beatrice. His writing, his faith, and his feelings for her all somehow were intertwined, in such a way that his concentration on any one encouraged the development of the others.

WHAT HAS NEVER BEEN WRITTEN

The late 1280s was a busy time in Dante's life. He probably took part in the Battle of Campaldino, in which Florence sent forces to the aid of Siena, a Tuscan city that was warring with neighboring Arezzo. He and Gemma had four children together. Their three sons, Giovanni, Pietro, and Jacopo, were named after the disciples who witnessed the transfiguration of Jesus; on taking religious vows years later, their daughter, Antonia, adopted the name of Beatrice. The original Beatrice,

Dante's beloved, was married in 1287; she died two years later, on June 8, 1289.

Perhaps it was this death that informed Dante's decision to circulate the poems that he had written about Beatrice, including an explanation of each piece, among the friends and fellow poets who shared his ideas and interests. He called his collection the *Vita Nuova*— the "new life."

Dante discussed his book with Guido Cavalcanti, and to Cavalcanti he ultimately dedicated the entire work. Even though poems were now being written consistently in the common language, Latin was still considered the only language appropriate to serious prose work; but Cavalcanti supported Dante's decision to write in Italian not only the *poetry* of the new collection but the *commentaries* as well. The appearance of the *Vita Nuova*, then, was a major step forward for Italian prose, which never had been taken seriously before.

Although in some parts the *Vita Nuova* echoed Dante's conversations with Cavalcanti, its focus was the story of Dante's relationship with Beatrice, beginning with their first meetings.

The link that Dante himself had drawn in his sonnets, between Beatrice and the divine, was as important in literary terms as it was for him personally; the new perspective carried European poetry into the next stage of its thematic development. Until then, poets had never found much significance in the human emotions, and sacred writing and secular love poems had been two very distinct kinds of writing. Dante was the first to insist that human love was ultimately united with the same divine love that was believed to create order in the universe.

The implications of this symbolism were far-reaching and radical: Dante was suggesting that Christ himself was appearing to him through the person of Beatrice. Dante did not consider this point of view sacrilegious; in his mind, just as Christ had claimed to demonstrate God's love to human beings, so Beatrice confirmed for Dante everything he knew about love. Years later, when he wrote *The Divine Comedy*, Dante would treat these fledgling ideas more thoroughly.

Dante's readers were not comfortable with the idea of a young woman as a symbol of Christ. It is true that women enjoyed far more credit for their intellectual abilities in Dante's Italy than in other times and places in European history, but they were by no means thought the equal of men. The ubiquitous troubadour poems spoke of women as dangerous beings; loving a woman could all too easily tempt a man away from loving God. The Church of the day took the more extreme position that, very loosely stated, women were the source of sin and evil. Dante's poetry claimed just the opposite—that his love for a human woman strengthened his love for God—and, if his work had been more widely circulated, he might easily have found himself surrounded by accusations of heterodoxy and facing excommunication or even death.

As it was, though, apparently only Dante's close friends read the *Vita Nuova*. Ironically, the person who was the least happy with the new ideas was Dante's closest friend, Guido Cavalcanti, to whom the work was dedicated. Cavalcanti's own poetry portrayed love in almost completely negative terms, as a cause of bewilderment and confusion that violated destructively the sense of self. For Cavalcanti, the beloved was an illusion, a bewitching. She might appear beautiful, but she could never possess real truth or goodness. The beginning of the *Vita Nuova* almost seems to subscribe to the same ideas.

In any event, Beatrice's death in 1289 plunged Dante back into the self-doubt and despair that rang true to his friend. For a time, the two were united in their thinking. His work of the time exudes Cavalcanti's influence:

> Harsh is the torment of each sighing breath
> When thoughts recall to my despondent mind
> The one for whom my grieving heart is rent;
> And often when I'm pondering Death
> The colour leaves my cheeks, so sweet I find
> Anticipation of his blandishment.

A year later, Dante was still immersed in his grief. One day, he looked up to see whether anyone was watching him as he cried—a problematic incident—and his eyes met those of a beautiful woman who was looking down at him from a window above. She resembled Beatrice somewhat, and in the subsequent weeks her gentleness and compassion became a balm to his aching heart. He began to turn for comfort to this woman, to whom he refers in the *Vita Nuova* as "the gentle lady."

Cavalcanti must have approved of his friend's new interest, for women seem in his view to have been largely interchangeable. He himself had never been constant in love, so it would not be surprising if he had little patience with his friend's growing obsession with Beatrice.

It is reasonable to surmise that after the death of Beatrice, Cavalcanti considered Dante free at last to return his attention to other matters.

Instead, though, a dream of Beatrice changed Dante forever. In the *Vita Nuova*, Dante insists that the dream took place "almost at the ninth hour," in keeping with all the other nines that haunted Beatrice's life. Just as Beatrice was equated in Dante's mind with Christ, now he equated her with the number nine as well, since, he reasoned, the square root of nine is three, which is the number of the Holy Trinity. Again, such reasoning may seem farfetched and convoluted to modern readers, but to Dante it was only further proof of Beatrice's divine significance.

In Dante's dream, Beatrice was once more not quite nine years old, just as was the first time he saw her. She was dressed in the same soft red dress, and he realized that something about her being would always be eternal, unchanged by death. Even death cannot conquer love, he understood now, and he turned his attention away from his "gentle lady" and vowed to be faithful to Beatrice.

Again, he expressed his new thoughts in sonnets, which he included in the *Vita Nuova*. But then he experienced another dream—or vision—of Beatrice, and this experience was so intense and significant for Dante that he resolved to write no more poetry about Beatrice until he had honed his skill. "And to this end," he wrote at the end of the *Vita Nuova*, "I apply myself as much as I can.... Thus, if it shall please Him by whom all things live that my life continue for a few years, I hope to compose concerning her what has never been written in rhyme of any woman."

ACADEMICS AND POLITICS

In his quest for literary self-improvement, for worthiness to write of his love, Dante turned his attention to the study of philosophy in the medieval sense—astronomy, geography, physiology, logic, metaphysics, and any other subdomain pursued by lovers of knowledge. He had a particularly strong attraction to astronomy.

The writing of two authors of antiquity, Cicero and Boethius, also inspired him. He was so excited by the depth and scope of the new ideas he encountered in their Latin works that he now began to think of philosophy, too, as a *donna gentile*—a replacement for the "gentle lady" of the *Vita Nuova*, but one who would support his love of Beatrice rather than distract him from it. For the next two years, from 1291 to 1293, he sought philosophical teaching and discussion wherever it could be found.

He had begun his studies looking for solace in his mourning for Beatrice, but he found far more. In his next lengthy literary work, the *Convivio*, he explained that just as someone who goes looking for silver may unexpectedly discover gold, so did he find in his philosophical pursuits something greater than simple comfort. Philosophy taught him a new way of thinking about truth.

Inspired by his new appreciation for philosophy, Dante now began to attend the religious schools run by the Franciscan and Dominican friars in the churches of Santa Croce and Santa Maria Novella, schools that offered instruction on a variety of subjects and permitted laymen to attend. In fact, unlike the monastic orders that withdrew from the world, early medieval friars such as these established their communities in cities for the very purpose of offering learning to the common man.

The teaching offered in the schools Dante now attended focused on ancient Greek and Arabic writings, primarily those of Aristotle and Avicenna. The Franciscans and Dominicans were considered radical when they offered the teachings of these men, for earlier in the thirteenth century the Church had officially condemned the works of both. Neither of these great ancient thinkers, of course, had been Christian; they had no orthodox belief in the immortal soul, and they viewed the universe as eternal and uncreated, or created without intention, rather than dependent on any single God. All serious scholars studied these works anyway, but it was often behind closed doors. Dante enjoyed the challenge, throwing himself into his studies with the obsession he had felt for Beatrice during her life. He spent so much time reading, in fact, that for some time he suffered from blurred vision and inflammation of the eyes.

Although his most famous work was yet before him, during this decade of his life Dante continued to explore poetic styles and techniques. He composed a group of sonnets far more ribald than the verse of the *Vita Nuova*. These were part of a correspondence with Dante's friend Forese Donati, a cousin of Gemma and fellow poet who would later become a character in *The Divine Comedy*. The writings the two men exchanged were full of low-grade mockery—Dante accused Donati of gluttony, and Donati mocked Dante's poverty. No evidence has been uncovered of a real quarrel between the two; still, critics have often been uncomfortable with the earthy humor of these sonnets, which seems very much at odds with the predominantly spiritual tone of Dante's other work. At the time, though, both kinds of poetry were popular: the intellectual and idealistic and the bawdy and hilarious. Perhaps Dante was merely trying his hand at another literary form, expanding his skills, or following his kinsman's lead—or perhaps he enjoyed the brief escapade into low humor.

Dante, as modern criticism understands him, would have seen no contradiction between these two popular poetic forms as his studies in philosophy progressed. The many theologians and philosophers of the time who saw the world as a duality, split into the material and the spiritual, believed that the body was at war with the spirit; it was the human body, these thinkers reasoned, that tempted human beings to sin. Dante seems to have disagreed. To him, the physical world and the spiritual world were connected, not at odds—so writing a coarse joke in verse did not distance him from God.

During these years, Dante also tried his hand at writing yet another form of poetry: his *rime petrose*, or "stony poems." True, throughout these rhymes Dante repeatedly uses some form of the word stone; but he meant the compositions to be impenetrable as well, so obscure and complex as to defy comprehension. Also, the subject matter was harsh, even violent, and he chose words studded with hard consonants, giving the verses a rough, rocky sound. These poems are very different from everything else Dante produced.

And this with reason: he had entered this decade of his life with the intention of growing as a poet, in order to express more adeptly the ideas that centered on Beatrice. By testing new forms of poetry like off-color verse and the *rime petrose*, Dante was expanding his poetic skill. His eventual masterpiece, *The Divine Comedy*, would incorporate aspects of all these forms. These poems seem not to have been intended as autobiographical, as the *Vita Nuova* had been, or theological, or philosophical. They were exercises that facilitated his evolution as a poet.

As Dante grew older, though, he could no longer dedicate himself so obsessively to his studies and his writing; he became involved to an ever greater extent in the ordinary affairs of daily life. As the head of a family and a connected member of the middle class, he had growing responsibilities to support his wife, children, and position. And he was becoming increasingly drawn into his city's charged political life.

In the early middle ages, the most intellectual and educated men were considered the best candidates for political office, and these usually were poets of one breed or another. We can assume that Dante learned civic duty from both Brunetto Latini and Guido Cavalcanti, as well as from his classical studies—but whatever the reason, Dante officially entered politics in November of 1295, at 30 years of age, when he became a member of the Special Council of the *Capitano del Popolo*. Florence had just begun a system of rule by six *priori*, or priors, chosen at two-month intervals from the six divisions of the city; this system of division would remain in place for some sixty years. Beneath the priors were two leading officials: the *Podesta*, or chief magistrate, and the *Capitano del Popolo*. Each official was aided by two councils, and Dante became a member of one of these.

These governing bodies were mostly made up of middle-class merchants and were fairly democratic in nature. One out of every 36 businessmen in Florence would eventually serve a six-month period on one of the advisory councils. Technically, only a member of a guild—roughly, the medieval form of the modern workers' union—could be a council member, but apparently many members of the aristocracy joined a guild for the very reason of entering politics. This is apparently what Dante did as well: he joined the Guild of Physicians and Apothecaries so as to qualify for political life. Dante had little interest in trade, but this guild was considered one of the most intellectual in the city, and Dante was interested in the field of medicine. By joining the guild, he would also be able to learn more about the sciences from its other members.

Dante's first six-month term of office shows no record of his making any special contribution to the council's decisions, but his opinions must have been valued even at this early stage in his political career, as he was chosen to be part of a special and powerful committee. Later, when he had completed this term of office, Dante was elected to serve on one of the other governing councils. He is known to have made a speech during his time in this office urging that measures be taken to ensure peace within the city's streets.

Throughout the decade, Dante remained active in political life in Florence. His positions, however, all were unpaid, so they did nothing to improve his financial outlook. His father had died in 1283, leaving to him and his stepbrother, Francesco, a modest fortune; but by this time both brothers were so short of money that they often had to take out loans. Eventually, Francesco became a successful businessman, but

Dante had no interest in business, and his finances were always uncertain. Despite his poverty, however, Florence considered him to be a member of a small elite circle of intellectual politicians, and although he also lacked any powerful family connections, his reputation continued to grow.

As Dante rose in political power, however, his role in the ongoing feud between the Guelphs and the Ghibellines also became more visible and put him in a dangerous position. Although technically the guilds possessed the governing power in Florence, a political society controlled by the Guelph family had enormous influence in the city's day-to-day politics. This society was very wealthy; it not only had the backing of many prominent bankers and merchants but also had taken over the property of its Ghibelline enemies at the time of their exile, several years earlier. The Guelph society used its wealth to control the city's politics by making loans to the priors—loans dependent, of course, on rule according to the Guelphs' wishes.

Although the Guelphs had been victorious over their old enemy the Ghibellines, they now began to fight among themselves with the same tenacity. They split into two factions: the Black Guelphs, led by Corso Donati, and the White Guelphs, led by Vieri de'Cerchi.

The Donati and Cerchi families were aristocrats who lived in the same section of the city; in fact, they were close neighbors. The Donati family, however, was older, with a longer history of aristocracy, while the Cerchi family was far more wealthy. This difference between the two families may help to explain the tension, but their feud began simply because Corso Donati and Vieri de'Cerchi did not like each other personally. Over the years, their antipathy grew until it affected the life of the entire city.

Dante's friend Guido Cavalcanti had long been a supporter of the Cerchi family, the White Guelphs. A few years earlier, Corso Donati had tried to have Cavalcanti murdered while he was on a pilgrimage to a Spanish shrine. The attempt on Cavalcanti's life failed, but when he returned to Florence he attacked Corso in the street. Donati supporters fought him off by hurling stones at him; Cavalcanti got away with only minor injuries, but he was fined 1,200 florins for his attack. Violence of this sort was a constant occurrence in the streets of Florence—perhaps inspiring Dante's speech on the need to ensure safety.

As the tensions mounted, the political differences between the two parties grew as well. The Black Guelphs supported the rule of the pope and France's House of Anjou (an important power in thirteenth-century Italy), while the Whites believed that Florence should be able to function independently, with no interference from these higher authorities. These were not merely ideological differences. Many of the Blacks had business interests both in Naples, which was ruled by Charles II, Count of Anjou, and in France itself. Of course, they favored a continued close relationship with the French. The Whites, on the other hand, had business dealings in other parts of Italy, so it was in their economic interest to distance themselves from French rule.

At first Dante did not side with either group. His wife was of the Donati family, and he had a strong relationship with Corso Donati's brother Forese. But he also was close with Guido Cavalcanti, a devoted supporter of the Cerchi. For some years, Dante managed diplomatically to avoid extremes and to offend no one, but this changed in 1300, when Dante was 35.

In that year, Pope Boniface VIII celebrated the new century by declaring it a Year of Jubilee and encouraged pilgrims to come to Rome, where he would forgive all their sins if they visited the churches of St. Peter and St. Paul a specified number of times. Dante may have been one of the many pilgrims who crowded the streets of Rome, particularly at Easter.

Politically, the year had begun calmly enough. At the end of 1299, Corso Donati had been implicated in a major financial scandal, and as a result Dante and the other priors had exiled him from the city—perhaps in the interest of peace. The citizens of Florence hoped that the departure of these two hot tempers would reduce the tension in Florentine streets.

But Pope Boniface offered his protection to Donati. He even went so far as to make Donati the *podesta* of a small town north of Rome. From there, Donati continued to exert his influence over Florence, and as the first months of the new century went by, Black-White tensions began to mount again. This time, though, Boniface himself became increasingly involved.

Florence's priors took action against some Florentine businessmen who were also residents of the pope's courts. The priors accused these men of conspiring against their native city and saw them sentenced to heavy fines; they were also to have their tongues cut out when they returned to Florence. As it happened, the businessmen were allies of Corso Donati as well.

The pope tried to have the sentence annulled. When he was unsuccessful, the anger between the Black Guelphs and the White Guelphs flared. At a May Day ball, young supporters of the two factions turned the dancing into brawling. A few weeks later, the Blacks organized a rally at the Church of Santa Trinita.

On that same May, Dante was trusted with a diplomatic mission when he was sent to a nearby city to raise support for the White Guelphs. While he was gone, the priors sentenced Corso Donati to death and ordered the destruction of his property. This sentence did nothing to calm the tension in Florence's streets. Pope Boniface sent one of his cardinals to Florence to work for peace—and promote the interests of the Black Guelphs—but this church official met with no success.

The priors were now at the end of their six-month term of office, and in June, Dante was one of the six new priors elected to office. Eight days after he assumed office, on the eve of the Feast of St. John the Baptist, another of the city's celebrations turned into a street brawl.

This time the fighting was not between Blacks and Whites, but between aristocrats and guild members. The response from Dante and his fellow priors was almost immediate: they banished several aristocratic families. They sent seven White leaders and their families in one direction and eight Blacks and their households in another. Dante's own closest friend, Guido Cavalcanti, was one of the Whites exiled from Florence. This must have caused Dante a great deal of personal pain, but he agreed with the other five priors: firm action must be taken to bring peace to Florence's streets. The violence could not be allowed to continue.

The White families who had been banished cooperated with the priors' ruling and left the city peacefully. The Black families, however, refused to leave for another two months.

By tradition, the priors elected in June held office for only two months, so Dante's term of office was soon over. As one of their first actions, the priors that replaced him and his colleagues reversed the banishment of the Whites. The Blacks' sentence they allowed to stand, however. This show of favoritism incensed both the Blacks and their supporter, Pope Boniface. Corso Donati, still under sentence of death, was biding his time.

DANTE IN EXILE

In the early years of the new century, Dante continued to be politically active. Now, though, he no longer kept a low profile in the Black-White controversies. In his speeches to the various councils on which he served, he was outspoken in his support of the White Guelphs, and he recommended that determined action be taken against Pope Boniface and other Black sympathizers. As result, he made some powerful enemies.

In the fall of 1301, Dante was sent on yet another diplomatic mission. This time he went to Pope Boniface himself, hoping to persuade the pope to step out of Florence's politics.

In the Middle Ages, the pope had as much power as any king. Although there were wise popes, many were corrupt and used their power to promote their own interests. Pope Boniface was one of the more controversial popes. People had many doubts about him, partly because of the way in which he had come into office in the first place.

The pope before Boniface was Celestine V, or Peter Morrone. At the time Morrone was elected to be pope, he was a hermit of nearly 80 years in age. Despite his acknowledged holiness, he lacked the education and experience necessary to an office so political as the medieval papacy, and the cardinals who had chosen him were soon appalled and concerned by his lack of sophistication. Morrone himself was desperately unhappy and wanted only to return to the quiet of his hermitage in the Abruzzi hills. Everyone was relieved when he at last resigned, after only four or five months on the throne, and left Rome.

Boniface took his place, but rumors spread about him. Some said that Morrone had been persuaded to resign through deception and trickery. One gossiper claimed that someone had stuck a tube through the wall of Morrone's room during the night and then spoken to him through it, claiming to be an angel sent by God to tell him to step down from the papal office. This rumor eventually became widespread, although today historians doubt that Boniface would have actually used such unsophisticated methods to achieve his ends. However, he may very well have taken advantage of Morrone's lack of experience in some way, using it to pressure Morrone to resign. When Morrone died a few years later, the rumors circulated once more; this time, the gossips claimed that Boniface had murdered the old man to remove any threat of his ever returning to claim his title. What is certain is that Boniface, the former Cardinal Gaetani, had at last imprisoned the old man, in a castle near Anagni.

Pope Boniface VIII was ambitious and ruthless. He was well aware of how important Florence was commercially and financially, and he was fiercely opposed to the independence that the White Guelphs claimed for their city. After all, an independent Florence would do him little good. He said of the Florentines, "I know their rights well enough, for they are usurers, and their lives are at the Church's disposal." Furious at the rebellion expressed by Florentines like Dante, Boniface turned to France's royal family to help him oust the White Guelphs from power.

When the House of Anjou actually sent 500 knights to Italy, the Whites began to be worried. They realized that the Blacks were eager for revenge; if the Donati were supported by outside military intervention, the Whites were in very real danger. Desperate to avert the threat to their party, they sent Dante and two other ambassadors to try to appease Pope Boniface.

The reception they received from the pope was not promising. "Why are you so stubborn?" he asked them. "Humble yourselves before me; and I tell you in truth that my only intention is for your city to be at peace. Two of you will go back, and may they have my blessing if they can ensure that my will is obeyed." Boniface kept Dante with him, no doubt fearing that Dante was too outspoken, too good with words, and too resolute in his support of the White faction.

Back in Florence, the city leaders were still trying to work out some kind of peace, but things were falling apart. By the end of October, the French forces entered the city. On their heals came Corso Donati and the other exiled Blacks. The Blacks released the political prisoners, and then they rioted through the streets.

For five days, the Blacks burned and pillaged the property of White Guelphs. Dante's house was one of those attacked. The six priors ruling at the time offered to step down, so that they could be replaced by a new governing force made up of three Black priors and three White priors. This was not enough for the Blacks; they overthrew the government completely and put Black leaders in their place.

Pope Boniface sent one of his cardinals to represent his own interests. He did not want the Blacks' alliance with the French to be so strong that they might rebel against his authority as well. The cardinal arrived on December 15th to find the city full of death and destruction. As Christmas Day approached, the Donati and Cerchi families seemed increasingly busy warring with each other. Dante was fortunate to be out of Florence, away from the violence.

But he could not escape the result of this new shift in power. On January 27, 1302, he was condemned *in absentia* of financial corruption, of opposing the French royalty and Pope Boniface, and of conniving against the Black Guelphs (who were described as "loyal devotees of the ... Church"). Dante was not guilty of any financial corruption, but he had been outspoken on the other two counts.

Dante's sentence was harsh. He was fined 5,000 florins and could never hold public office in Florence again. Furthermore, he was banished from the city for two years. To complicate matters, the new Black ruler decreed that if Dante did not appear within three days and justify himself, if he could, and pay his fine, his property in Florence would be destroyed. Since Dante was not even in the city and had no way of knowing about his sentence until later, he failed to appear.

A few months later, Dante and other White supporters received even stiffer sentences. The Black ruler now made them permanent exiles from Florence—under penalty of death by fire. Dante never returned. Perhaps occupied with Florentine politics, Dante produced no known works in the early years of the new century; but much later he would treat exile briefly in *The Divine Comedy*:

> You will leave behind all that you have loved
> Most dearly, and this is the arrow
> The bow of exile shoots first.
> You will find out how salty
> Someone else's bread tastes, and how is the way
> Up and down another's stairs.

At first, the exiled Dante stayed in Tuscany with the others, who, using sometimes diplomacy and sometimes military action, worked to bring an end to their banishment. Dante often acted as their spokesman. At times their cause seemed hopeful, but ultimately they were unsuccessful.

The exiled Whites had tried to use arbitration to accomplish their goals. Pope Benedict, Boniface's successor, had also sent his cardinal to negotiate for peace. Neither, however, had been successful. The Blacks continued to burn the property of the Whites, and eventually the cardinal conceded and left. The month after, Pope Benedict died. The

Whites could not predict what position Benedict's successor would take, and they were tired of negotiations that never seemed to accomplish anything. The exiles were frustrated and angry. They wanted to fight.

But Dante did not. The events of the past years had demonstrated all too well to him that military action accomplishes very little. The violence in Florence never brought peace; instead, it was self-feeding. New acts of warfare only inspired still greater military involvement. The fighting never ceased.

The other Whites were not interested in his perspective, however, and they launched an attack against Florence. Their action was disastrous; as many as 400 Whites and Ghibellines lost their lives in the fighting.

Dante felt he no longer had anything to contribute to the Whites' faction. He saw things differently than his old companions did—and they no longer listened to him or respected his wisdom. Later, he wrote in *The Divine Comedy*:

> And what will weigh most heavily on your shoulders
> Will be your wicked and foolish companions ...
> They will be utterly ungrateful, mad and evil
> Towards you; ...
> So you will have done well
> In becoming a party by yourself.

No one shared Dante's views on Florence's strife. Doubly exiled from all that he had once known, Dante left the Whites behind and headed north all alone. He had become a one-man political party.

Dante now relied on the hospitality of various nobles, and throughout his exile, he held administrative and diplomatic positions in their courts. When he left Tuscany, he found his first true refuge in the home of Can Grande della Scala, a noble of Verona. In Can Grande's home, Dante at last had enough peace and quiet to focus on his writing.

Can Grande was a Ghibelline, one of the Guelphs' old enemies, but in their exile the White Guelphs often found the Ghibellines sympathetic to their cause. Although Can Grande was a young man barely 20 years old when Dante came to live in his household, he was fast becoming one of the most powerful men in northern Italy. He was a skillful military commander, and for years he was undefeated in battle.

As a result, he brought under his control many cities in Lombardy and the northeast of Italy.

Can Grande was also noted for his hospitality and generosity. He gave many exiles their own comfortable apartments in his household. Dante admired him and was grateful for the refuge he found in Verona. He spent six years there.

During this time, Dante began working on two more works called the *Convivio* (*The Banquet*) and the *De Vulgari Eloquentia* (*On Eloquence in the Vernacular*). Both of these books were intended to teach Dante's learning and ideas to others. He wrote the *Convivio* in the Italian language that everyone could understand most easily, but he wrote *De Vulgari Eloquentia* in the more intellectual Latin. He never finished either work.

Although the *Vita Nuova* seems more concrete, the philosophy that Dante wrote in the *Convivio* is not so very different from his thoughts in his earlier work. Through his studies, he had explored his ideas about the nature of reality far more deeply, but the later book only extends the ideas of the *Vita Nuova* to a more abstract level.

In the *Convivio*, Dante based his ideas on the philosophy of past thinkers—like St. Augustine, Aristotle, and Virgil—as well as the ideas of theologians and thinkers who were his contemporaries, including St. Thomas Aquinas, St. Bonaventure, and Boethius. Dante intended the book to be a "banquet," an intellectual meal that would offer its readers food for their minds. The *Convivio* gives passionate praise to knowledge in and of itself. Dante refers to knowledge as the soul's ultimate perfection, the source of human beings' greatest happiness, "the bread of angels." In a world where he had lost most of the tangible possessions upon which he had once relied, Dante clung to something that circumstances could not take from him—his years of learning.

Dante not only used the ideas of other thinkers as his foundation, but he also imitated their style. As an outcast who had lost the acceptance and prestige that had once been his, Dante felt the need to justify his thoughts in a new way. Today's psychologists might say that Dante was experiencing disequilibrium; in other words, his current experiences were at odds with what he had learned about his place in the world in the past, and as a result his concept of his own identity was shaken and challenged. He wrote in the *Convivio*:

> From the time when the citizens of ... Florence saw fit to cast
> me away from her sweet bosom ... I have made my way
> through almost all the regions to which this language
> extends, a homeless wanderer, reduced almost to beggary,
> and showing against my will the wound inflicted by fortune,
> which is very often imputed unjustly to the one afflicted....
> Many have seen me in person who perhaps entertained a
> different image of me in virtue of a certain reputation I
> enjoyed, so that in their eyes not only do I myself lose in
> esteem, but all my works ... are cheapened.

Dante needed to construct a new self-image. To do so, he adopted a more learned style when he wrote the *Convivio*.

In the *Convivio*, Dante expressed his view that human beings from the time they are born are searching for God; God is the only thing that will ultimately satisfy human desires, but, said Dante, humans find God first in the ordinary details of existence. According to Dante, many people naturally become confused; they mistake physical satisfaction as an end in itself, rather than seeking it as the expression of God. But by the time people die, said Dante in the *Convivio*, they can anticipate eternal life with God the same way a merchant looks forward to going home when he is laden down with riches after a successful trading trip.

Since Dante wrote this thought when he had lost all material possessions, his words are a statement of faith. When Beatrice died, Dante had risen to the understanding that love is undiminished by death, since true love wants nothing for itself; now, in a similar way, his exile forced him to a new understanding of faith: physical loss cannot alter the nature of eternal reality.

Critics insist, however, that despite his efforts, during these years Dante never succeeded in completely making sense out of both his Christian faith and his philosophy. He never quite put the two together into one entire worldview. This may have been why he ultimately abandoned both the *Convivio* and the *De Vulgari Eloquentia*.

In both books, though, Dante argued that human beings must rise above their immediate circumstances and look at life from a more universal perspective. That higher perspective, he insisted, was the only true reality; our individual, subjective viewpoints are only illusions, because they do not grasp the whole picture.

Dante had intended the *Convivio* to have 15 books, but only four books survive; he had planned that *De vulgari eloquentia* would have four books, but he only completed two. Outside events interrupted Dante's writing, however. Word had arrived that Henry of Luxemburg was coming to Italy. Henry was soon to be crowned the Holy Roman Emperor, and Dante saw his coming as a sign of new hope.

The Monarchia

On May 1, 1308, Albert of Hapsburg, the Holy Roman Emperor, had been assassinated. Italy was a part of the Holy Roman Empire, but Albert's assassination meant little to most Italians. Dante had never even thought of Albert as the real emperor, for Albert had never been crowned by the pope or set foot on Italian soil.

Henry VII of Luxembourg, Albert's successor, planned to change all that. Not only would he come to Italy to be crowned by the pope, but he also had definite plans for the Italian city-states. He had every intention of transforming them into valuable military and political participants in the Empire.

The pope did not want to lose his own political power in Italy, but nevertheless he cautiously welcomed Henry to Italy, making clear all the same that Henry was not to interfere with the pope's influence over the city-states of central Italy. Clement and Henry agreed to hold a papal coronation in 1312.

Henry, however, had no intention of waiting so long. In the spring of 1310, he sent his ambassadors to northern Italy, announcing his intention of coming imminently to Italy to be crowned. The Emperor-elect intended to arrive no later than September, his ambassadors announced, and he expected the cities to be ready for his coming. As part of their preparations, they were to cease all fighting; a general truce was to be declared until November 1. Henry's ambassadors stressed that he had no intention of taking sides in the ongoing hostilities between the Guelphs and the Ghibellines. Rather, Henry would come to Italy to make peace.

Northern Italy welcomed Henry's arrival, but Tuscany, the region in which lay Florence, had misgivings about the new emperor. Florence in particular did not want to lose the power it enjoyed over the surrounding lands, and Florence's Black rulers feared that Henry might

force them to share the city's government with the exiled Whites. The
Blacks complied with Henry's wishes superficially, but in reality their
goals did not change.

Finally, early in October, Henry began his journey across the Alps
into Italy. His forces were not particularly large—he had only 5,000
men, and only 500 of these were mounted—and he was somewhat short
on funds. The journey continued smoothly for two months, and after
traveling through the northern Italian cities Henry reached Milan by
December 23.

Dante welcomed him with figurative open arms. He looked to
Henry as a savior, a second Moses come to deliver the people. To
encourage other Italians to see Henry's arrival from a similar point of
view, Dante began writing letters to be passed around Italy's cities. He
wrote thirteen epistles in total; many were hopeful and enthusiastic
letters that called for a new reign of peace in Italy.

The rulers of Florence did not share Dante's enthusiasm. They
began to impose conditions on Henry's rule—among others, that
Florence would retain all its lands and possessions exactly as they were.
In an effort to garner support for their position, they sent a letter of
appeal to the pope, pleading for his protection against Henry.

On January 6, 1311, Henry was at last crowned King of the
Romans by the Archbishop of Milan. Dignitaries from all regions of
Italy were there—but representatives from Tuscany's Guelph-ruled
cities were conspicuously absent. Still, the coronation was a splendid
celebration and lasted several days.

After only a month, however, uprisings against Henry began to
spread across Italy. Before Henry could deal with one rebellion, another
would spring up somewhere else. Florence was rumored to be behind at
least some of the fighting.

Dante was evidently furious—so furious, in fact, that some
historians question whether he may have become temporarily
unbalanced mentally. The letter he wrote in reaction to these acts of
rebellion was impassioned and extreme. Florence's citizens, he wrote,
were wicked, avaricious, arrogant; they would be punished for their
insolence, he predicted. Dante claimed that Henry was God's own
minister, a Christ-like figure. Those who reject him, raged Dante,
deserved to die. He prophesied that Henry would take Florence, driving
the Black rulers into an exile they richly deserved. Henry never did
succeed in taking Florence, and Dante's passionate letters fell on deaf

ears. The Blacks, more defiant than ever, organized a formal anti-imperial league.

Dante's next letter was to the Emperor himself. In it, he referred to Henry as the long-awaited Sun, the Lamb of God, and he called on the Emperor to attack Florence at once. If Florence were defeated, promised Dante, the rest of Italy would soon fall into line. No one knows whether Henry ever received Dante's letter or, if he did, why he failed to heed Dante's advice. For the remainder of 1311, Henry avoided Florence.

In the meantime, Florence had refused to receive Henry's ambassadors; in fact, the city had nearly murdered one of his delegates. Rebellions continued to break out in cities across Italy, and the plague had struck Genoa. Henry's own wife, Margaret, died from the plague on December 13. Overwhelmed, Henry formally banned Florence, depriving it of the right to self-government. The Florentines were officially declared to be rebels against the Empire. Political exiles like Dante were not included in this sentence.

Henry was determined to proceed to Rome, where he would have his third and final coronation as Emperor. Despite his official action against Florence, he continued to evade any direct military involvement with the city. In May, he arrived in Rome, hoping to receive the pope's official coronation.

Pope Clement was not in Rome, however, at the time of Henry's arrival. One of the cardinals did perform a ceremony, placing the crown on Henry's head, but Pope Clement was now open in his lack of support for the Emperor. Dante viewed this shift in policy as a betrayal. When he wrote *The Divine Comedy*, he portrayed Clement as the personification of corruption.

Soon after his final coronation, Henry at last moved toward Florence. His siege of the city began in mid-September and lasted for six weeks. Ultimately, he was never able to surround the city completely. During this time, Henry came down with malaria, which only weakened his position still more, but he was able to achieve some minor local victories. Florence perceived him as being dangerous enough that they did not want to risk fighting him in the open, outside the city walls.

By August of the following year, Henry marched south, intending first to go to Rome and then to attack Naples by land and sea. But he did not live long enough to accomplish his plans; he fell ill once more with malaria, and he died several weeks later. Dante joined Pisa and the imperial army in their deep sorrow for the dead Emperor. Florence rejoiced.

Although Henry was dead, Dante did not abandon his Imperial Dream. He hoped that a future emperor would succeed where Henry had failed. In Dante's mind, a monarchy was the only permanent answer to Italy's endless fighting.

Later, when his own life was settled enough that he could devote himself to his writing once more, Dante summarized his opinions in a book entitled *Monarchia*. In the *Convivio* he had also called for the necessity of a single world ruler in order to ensure peace and happiness, and now, in the *Monarchia*, he elaborated his beliefs still further.

According to the *Monarchia*, humanity can only achieve wisdom if it experiences peace; the emperor's job is to ensure this state of tranquility so that human knowledge can thrive. Worldwide unity is necessary, Dante stressed, so that society will be stable and efficient. The emperor must be the epitome of justice, protecting individual freedom.

The *Monarchia* also argues for the separation of church and state. The pope and the emperor should have separate jurisdictions: the Church should concern itself only with human beings' souls, while the state should deal with earthly concerns. The ideal emperor leads his subjects to temporal well-being; the ideal pope guides human beings to eternal life. The authority of the Church should be based primarily on the Bible and the writings of the Church Fathers; canon law should have no application to political affairs. Although the emperor should revere and respect the pope, his authority comes to him directly from God, rather than from the Church. His government should not be subordinate to the pope's. As the Church Father Justinian had written, the imperial eagle was also the "bird of God"; secular government, according to Dante, plays an essential role in human redemption.

The *Monarchia* is more idealistic philosophy than political study. Dante never provided many concrete details about the imperial order he imagined. Despite his own practical experience in government, he seemed to have little interest in explaining the actual workings of the government he envisioned.

Still, Dante's theories about government arose from his own experiences. His bitterness and disillusionment with Florence's years of strife and chaos inspired him to look to a monarchy as an answer. His own lonely years of exile made his beliefs that much stronger and passionate. Although he showed no interest in the details of actual government, Dante considered his political ideas to be a central part of the revelation he was called to make to the world, a core truth he was inspired to express. When he wrote his greatest opus, *The Divine Comedy*, he included his philosophies about the monarchy as a part of the divine scheme he presented.

Unlike any of Dante's previous works, though, *The Divine Comedy* was far greater in scope than any single aspect of human life. It covered the entire range of human experience.

Exactly when or where Dante worked on *The Divine Comedy*—a three-part journey through the afterlife divided into the *Inferno* (Hell), the *Purgatorio* (Purgatory), and the *Paradiso* (Heaven)—is uncertain. He began at some point late in his exile, perhaps during his years at Verona. In the previous years, as he drifted from one location to the next, his only home had been his own mind. Within the walls of his mental sanctuary, Dante began his long work, despite the external changes that ebbed and flowed around him. Writing the sacred poem made him thin, he claimed, perhaps because it took so much energy, particularly considering the circumstances of his life.

YEARS OF TRANQUILITY

In 1315, Dante was still in the midst of writing the early parts of *The Divine Comedy*. Meanwhile, the power of his patron Can Grande, as well as that of other Ghibellines, was continuing to grow. They had gained military support from Henry's old forces, and they were now a significant threat to Florence. The Black Guelphs were worried.

The Florentine rulers decided that the time had come to mollify some of their enemies. In an attempt to demonstrate an openness to reconciliation, they issued a series of amnesty proposals for the exiles. Dante was eventually included in these proposals.

The amnesties offered official pardon to the exiles—an amnesty contingent on their acceptance of certain conditions. Each would have to pay a fine. More humiliating, every exile must submit to an official ceremony, called the *oblatio*, in which criminals dressed in sackcloth and paper miters and processed from the prison to the baptistry, where they were offered publicly to God and John the Baptist. After participating in the degrading *oblatio*, the exiles would be incarcerated.

Dante's reaction to the proposal was immediate scorn. He poured out self-righteous anger in a letter addressed to "a Florentine friend." The terms of the amnesty, he made clear, were ridiculous. They failed to recognize his innocence, his years of hardship, or his intellectual effort and achievement. In short, they did not give Dante his due. As much as he longed for reconciliation with his home city, he refused to demean himself by accepting the Florentine rulers' terms. After all, he concluded in his letter, he could study philosophy and the stars anywhere; he did not need to go home to fulfill his calling in life. He closed his letter with these words: "Rest assured, I shall not want for bread."

Dante was still living comfortably in the household of Can Grande. Life there was luxurious and stimulating, and by this time Dante had become his patron's friend. To express his gratitude to Can Grande, Dante addressed his thirteenth and last epistle to his patron, praising Can Grande's goodness and discussing the *Paradiso*, also dedicated to Can Grande.

As much as Dante admired and appreciated Can Grande, however, he did not always feel at home in his household. Can Grande was first of all a great warlord, and he enjoyed sharing the rough pleasures of his troops. By this time, Dante's outlook on life was far more serious, and he apparently experienced a growing tension between himself and some of Can Grande's courtiers and soldiers. He longed for a quieter, more intellectual atmosphere where he could devote himself to his writing and his philosophy.

In 1318, Dante left Verona and settled down in the court of Guido Novello in Ravenna. Novello was himself a poet, and he offered Dante the stability and peace he needed to finish his great work.

The *Inferno* and the *Purgatorio* were already complete, and as these works became well known, a circle of other poets and literati gathered in Ravenna to discuss politics, philosophy, theology, and the sciences. Dante's wife and children—Gemma Donati and Peter, James, and Antonia—also joined him at Ravenna.

THE *QUAESTIO* AND THE *ECLOGUES*

While not working on *The Divine Comedy*, Dante also wrote two other works, now considered minor or less important. One of these was the *Quaestio de aqua et terra*, a short prose work about the relative positions of earth and water in our world.

The mainly Ptolemaic philosophy of Dante's day conceived of the universe as a series of concentric circles, with the Earth at the center. Dante followed this paradigm when he wrote the *Paradiso*. The physical hierarchy was a reflection of the spiritual hierarchy that medieval thinkers believed real. The earth was thought to consist of four elemental spheres—fire, air, water, and earth, with earth being at the center. But this orderly concept of the world was destabilized by examples of land's protruding from water and creating large areas of earth-surface not covered by water's sphere. The question became one of whether sea level could ever be lower than a piece of land. Using the medieval tools of logic and dialectic, Dante confidently answered this question in the *Quaestio*: No, the sea is at no point higher than dry land. He attributes the presence of dry land to the Heaven of the Fixed Stars, whose power has "drawn out" the land from beneath the ocean's surface as part of the divine plan for human life.

Dante presented the *Quaestio* in the church of Santa Elena in Verona on January 20, 1320. All the intelligentsia of Verona were there on that Sunday to hear Dante's words. Dante closed his lecture with these words: "I, Dante Alighieri, the least among philosophers have resolved this question in the fair city of Verona in the presence of nearly all its men of learning—save a few, over-endowed with charity and humility, who have felt unable to attend."

The *Eclogues* were the last poetry Dante wrote. These Latin poems were part of his correspondence with Giovanni del Virgilio, the Chair of Latin Poetry at Bologna University. Virgilio's first letter complained to Dante that *The Divine Comedy* should not have been written in everyday Italian; if Dante were to write a Latin epic instead, said Giovanni, his fame would be worldwide, rather than limited to only Italy. Giovanni closed his letter with some well-intentioned flattery: in comparison to Dante, he said, he was but a goose cackling to a swan.

Although Dante was in the midst of writing the *Paradiso*, he enjoyed the diversion of answering Giovanni's letter. Instead of writing a Latin epic, however, he wrote an eclogue—a pastoral poem that conceal a moral or political message in the affairs of shepherds—a form of poetry that had not been used since antiquity. Dante portrayed himself and all his friends, including Giovanni, as shepherds.

Giovanni responded with an eclogue of his own in the following spring, and a year later Dante wrote a second. Dante clearly enjoyed both these little exercises, which became a form of sparring; there is no reason to believe the engagement between the two friends was anything but good-natured.

THE LAST MISSION

Dante completed the final book of *The Divine Comedy* by 1321. In that same year, in late July or early August, Dante traveled to Venice on a diplomatic mission for Guido Novello. Tension between Venice and Ravenna had been growing because of a dispute over custom fees on trade between the two cities. The two forces had clashed several times on the Adriatic Sea, and Ravenna's ships had done well against the Venetian crafts; Venice's hostility had increased correspondingly, and by the time of the mission war had become a very real possibility. Cavalcanti sent his ambassadors on a mission of peace.

According to some early historians, Dante was scheduled to speak on behalf of Ravenna, but the Venetians, wary of his eloquence, refused to allow it. They further refused to provide his transportation back to Ravenna by ship, for fear that he would persuade the admiral of their fleet to question his loyalties. Dante was constrained to travel home by land, and on the way, through marshy, mosquitoed lands, he contracted malaria. He probably survived to reach Ravenna, but in mid-September he at last succumbed and was buried ceremoniously in Ravenna. Giovanni del Virgilio composed his epitaph:

> Here lies the theologian Dante, well versed in every branch of learning that philosophy may nurture in her shining bosom, the glory of the Muses, and an author loved by the unlearned: with his fame he strikes both poles. It is he who assigned the dead to their places and defined the roles of the twin swords [i.e., the Empire and the Papacy], and this both in Italian and Latin. Most recently he was playing his Pierian pipes in the pastures; but envious Atropos, alas, cut short that joyous work. Ungrateful Florence, a cruel fatherland, rewarded her bard with bittern fruit of exile; but compassionate Ravenna is glad to have received him in the bosom of Guido Novello, its revered leader. In the year of Our Lord one thousand three hundred and thrice seven, on the Ides of September, then did he return to his stars.

By the end of the 14th century, the *Comedy* was read aloud throughout Italy like a sacred text, and Florence became eager to atone for its past sins; but Ravenna refused to surrender the bones of its national hero. Dante's grave remains in Ravenna today, despite a half-millennium of Florentine attempts at relocation.

In fact, in the 17th century the conflict over Dante's remains became so fierce that Franciscan monks in Ravenna were motivated to remove the bones from the sarcophagus and hide them. They were placed in a small wooden coffin that was then bricked into the wall of a small chapel and remained there until its discovery by workmen in May of 1865. After careful study, the discovered remains were translated to a lead-covered walnut coffin and then finally returned to the original sarcophagus.

The Italian city-states had recently united into one nation—a major step toward the peace and solidarity that Dante had advocated in the *Monarchio*. Ravenna now could lay claim to Dante's body in the name of a new nation; surely, Dante would have been pleased.

ELIZABETH A.S. BEAUDIN

Dante: Imagining Salvation

In the second half of the 20th century, the American poet James Merrill won the Pulitzer Prize for his collection of poems *Divine Comedies*. In Buenos Aires a few decades earlier, Jorge Luis Borges had earned the attention of an international audience by writing of a fellow who imagines a universe under the cellar steps while mourning the loss of his beloved Beatriz. Centuries earlier, Cervantes and Shakespeare had created, respectively, the wanderings of Don Quixote, and *Hamlet*, *King Lear*, and *Macbeth*. Yet some three hundred years before these two set the standard in novel and drama, Dante Alighieri was composing his encyclopedic vision of the human journey through wretchedness to blessedness. The first part first of this vast undertaking appeared in 1315, and the second and third parts began to circulate years later; and between 1330 and 1348, manuscripts were commissioned and copied of the entire work that today we call *The Divine Comedy*.

The poem includes some 14,233 verses in *terza rima*,[1] spanning 100 cantos that Dante organized thematically and structurally into the *Inferno*, the *Purgatorio*, and the *Paradiso*—Hell, Purgatory, and Paradise. Strangely enough, Dante refers to it as a *commedia* [2] and only twice; critically, then, the title is one of innumerable elements discussed in Dante scholarship over the centuries. It presented a problem immediately, for comedy as a genre implied a specific mode of writing. By

---

Citations are from Alighieri, Dante. *The Divine Comedy*. Charles S. Singleton, ed. and trans. Bollingen Series. Princeton: Princeton University Press, 1970.

medieval definitions, whereas tragedy was the story in high language of the fates of exalted characters, a comedy's language was low, often ribald, and its characters were from the lower classes. Dante's work evidently broke with these generic definitions, as his poem offered a rich panorama of characters and accompanying emotions and his language was equally varied and lush; but a case can be made that *The Divine Comedy* is indeed more comic than tragic; it ends happily. The overall tenor of Dante's epic poem points to its comprehensiveness in content and flexibility in execution, and it is clear from the poem's scope that Dante's "comedy" was the product of much contemplation and demonstrated a keen awareness of its eventual audience. For the modern reader, as well as her medieval counterpart, the three canticles act as a roadmap to follow as Dante interprets moral justice, poetics, philosophy, and theology.

His readers were quick to call Dante "the Divine Poet," even though the adjective *Divina* was not added to the title of the work until the appearance of a 1555 Venetian edition prepared by Gabriele Giolito. For Dante, the epithet was most likely of little consequence in comparison to his determination to figure poets—including himself—philosophers, sinners and saints throughout *The Divine Comedy*. The diversity of names, recognizable to Dante's contemporary audience as well as to readers today, served Dante's purpose of bringing his journey closer to his reader's reality while at the same time adding layers of authority to his text.

Dante set his authority quite high. His is a divinely inspired project, one in which Dante doubles his presence, acting as both poet and pilgrim. The guides accompanying Dante-pilgrim serve his exalted calling. Indeed, Dante's escort throughout the most arduous part of the journey is Virgil, author of the *Aeneid* and a figure of great poetic tradition. Virgil, on the intercession of Beatrice, Dante's greatest inspiration, appears to the fallen and frightened Dante-pilgrim in the opening scenes. These two points of light in Dante-poet's life—Virgil and his poetic inspiration along with Beatrice and her poetic powers—guide Dante-pilgrim in one form or another in the Poet's quest to envision bliss.

The presence of Beatrice—whether directly as a character or implied as a motivating force—is uninterrupted throughout *The Divine Comedy*. Virgil, the guide Dante-poet imagines, works as her instrument in two of the three canticles. By the details given in *Inf* 1.67–75, the

Virgil-guide would have been very recognizable as the Mantuan author of the *Eclogues*; the character, then, had existences both poetic and empirical. The doubling that is present in Dante—he wears the hats of both poet and character—is simulated again in Virgil and Beatrice. The interplay of fictional and real existences allows Dante to conflate allegory and realism into his own vision of the two. At the same time, the resulting fusion heralds encyclopedic layerings of perspectives and ideas, which Dante will introduce throughout the poem.

Much critical attention has been paid to this tension between allegory and realism in the work. In the opening scene of the *Comedy*, Dante is forgetful because he is "full of sleep" and cannot remember how he entered the "dark wood." (*Inf.* 1.1–11) Later, in his encounter with Francesca, Dante is so overcome with pity that he faints. (*Inf.* 5.140–142) In reality, his readers would understand these emotions. On an allegorical plane, forgetting, falling, and fainting serve Dante's higher intention of preparing the reader for the many, often confrontational, ideas that constitute the journey. Scholars today in one way or another incorporate into their readings of these exemplary scenes not only the medieval and Renaissance commentaries but also, and especially, the heritage of criticism from the early and mid-20th century. The resulting historiography resembles the many layers of authority that Dante himself incorporates into his poem.

In *Mimesis*, Erich Auerbach refers to Dante's fusion of realism and allegory as "figural realism," basing his argument on Christian typology and exegesis. He emphasizes Virgil and Beatrice in particular to explain his point:

> ... [T]heir appearance in the other world is a fulfillment of their appearance on earth, their earthly appearance a figure of their appearance in the other world. I stressed the fact that a figural schema permits both its poles—the figure and its fulfillment—to retain the characteristics of concrete historical reality, in contradistinction to what obtains with symbolic or allegorical personifications, so that figure and fulfillment—although one 'signifies' the other—have a significance which is not incompatible with their being real. (195)

Charles Singleton argues that the allegorical roles of Beatrice and Virgil transferred the historical or real to the fictional and higher plane. His comments imply further critical distillation of (or disagreement with) earlier scholars, such as Benedetto Croce and Francesco De Sanctis. The Singletonian stamp on later discussions of allegory and the *Comedy* sprang from his emphasis on the difference between "allegory of poets" and "allegory of theologians," in other words, those who create and those who interpret. In "Two Kinds of Allegory," suggesting a preference for the "allegory of theologians," Singleton cites the explanation of allegory found in the *Epistle to Can Grande della Scala*, attributed to Dante, which states:

> ... [W]e see clearly that the subject round which the alternative senses play must be twofold. And we must therefore consider the subject of this work as literally understood, and then its subject as allegorically intended ... (14)

Enrst Curtius carefully studied the earlier scholarship of the *Vita Nuova*, but disparaged its conclusions, believing that it privileged the real Beatrice to excess. Instead—carrying his interpretation beyond the boundaries of 19th-century readings by suggesting the mythic and apocalyptic expanses of Dante's own project—he maintains:

> ... Dante believed that he had an apocalyptic mission. This must be taken into consideration in interpreting him. Hence the question of Beatrice is not mere idle curiosity. Dante's system is built up in the first two cantos of the *Inferno*, it supports the entire *Commedia*. Beatrice can be seen only within it.... Exegesis is also bound to leave their full weight to all the passages at the end of the *Purgatorio* and in the *Paradiso* which are opposed to the identification of Beatrice with the daughter of the banker Portinari. Beatrice is a myth created by Dante. (377)

Whether today's scholarship privileges one earlier theory or another, what remains clear in the work is that Dante employed decorum or *convenientia* as his guidebook when manipulating the dualities of realism and allegory. In other words, Dante pursued a balance of propriety between event and situations, characters and message, for the sake of his higher mission. Thus, as *The Divine Comedy* opens, both Virgil and Beatrice are present. Virgil awakens Dante in the "dark wood."[3] Allegorically, Virgil-poet accompanies Dante-poet in creating his poem of sin, punishment, repentance and redemption.[4] Still, even though Dante-pilgrim calls his escort "My Master," Virgil can accompany Dante only so far. It is Beatrice the theologian, not merely the love-object of Dante's past, who will enlighten and empower Dante-poet, through reprimands, scholastic commentaries, and philosophical debates. Her vision, founded on the highest authority, will bring Dante to his divine objective.

Dante conceived of the path to redemption as progressing through three territories, three structural and thematic units, or canticles. Overall, these three comprise 100 *cantos*, a form characteristic of an epic or narrative poem. The first canticle, the *Inferno*, contains 34 cantos, one of which is an introduction. Each of the second and third canticles, the *Purgatorio* and the *Paradiso*, contains 33 cantos. Numbering—of cantos, verses, verse forms, characters, and events—repeatedly plays a significant role throughout the work both in its content and structure, as it did in Dante's real-life understanding of his interactions with his flesh-and-blood Beatrice.

The poem's division into three parts mirrors its thematic content: a Florentine poet aged about 35, named Dante, gives a first-person narrative of a divinely ordered journey through the three worlds of the afterlife. There are three guides: Virgil, Beatrice, and, at the very end, Bernard of Clairvaux. The journey takes place in the spring of 1300, culminating in Paradise on Easter Sunday.[5] The three divisions of *The Divine Comedy* are consistent with three moral themes: sinners, sinful dispositions, and examples of virtue. Dante refers to his epic at one point as his "*poema sacro*," sacred because it comes into being by God's wish. (*Par.* 25.1) Since his work is divinely inspired, Dante utilizes whatever he finds appropriate or fitting to meet his goal. His avowed mission is to find the straight path and redeem his eternal soul. (*Inf.* 1.3) Dante believes it is fitting to share his struggle with his readership. As the pilgrim's expedition proceeds, the reader perceives that the placement of souls within the tripartite structure is proportionate to their disposition. In other words, individuals reside in the three worlds as a result of an active choice of will. The term *contrapasso*,[6] based on the principle of justice set forth by St. Thomas Aquinas in his *Summa Theologica*, describes Dante's sense of moral justice and the appropriateness of placement and fate. Although Dante mentions the term only once (*Inf.* 28.142), the degree of suffering in Hell and Purgatory and the distance from the perfection of God in Paradise illustrate *contrapasso* and lends structure to Dante's poem.

The *Inferno*, the first division of *The Divine Comedy*, offers the most compelling and horrifying examples of *contrapasso* as Dante describes his interpretation of Hell and its occupants. In Dante's imagination, Hell is conical in shape and starts from a point directly below Jerusalem and then descends to the center of the Earth. As one moves down through the 10 levels (the entrance and the 9 circles), thus putting more distance between oneself and God, Hell becomes ever more horrific. Dante first conveys his sense of fear at the thought of the arduous journey ahead. His pulse trembles; he is racked with doubt and weeps in front of Virgil, who replies that the journey is vital if Dante is to find his way. Surprisingly, Virgil's admonitions are not sufficiently persuasive. To convince Dante that there is no other path to salvation, he must revert to stronger tactics. He relates words spoken by Dante's beloved Beatrice:

> Go now, and with your fair speech and with whatever is needful for his deliverance, assist him so that it may console me. I am Beatrice who send you. I come from a place to which I long to return. Love moved me and makes me speak. (*Inf.* 2.67–72)

Beatrice's higher Love transcends the limited role given to Dante's former love object and here acquires a voice. In turn, she verbalizes what Dante will illustrate in the three books of his poem: "fair speech" is required for deliverance. As Virgil explains, if he is to envision the blessedness of salvation, the pilgrim must see all the horrors that lie ahead. If Dante is to complete his divinely inspired mission, he must put speech to these visions so his readers can perceive them as well.

At the edge of Hell, Virgil shows Dante the first group of inhabitants called the Neutrals who neither chose commendable behavior nor committed grave sins. Once Charon ferries them over the Acheron, Dante and Virgil reach the first circle: Limbo. Dante sees infants and virtuous non-Christians who dwell in this place of sighs and wailing because they were never cleansed of original sin, the reason they will never see God. This too is where Virgil resides, as well as the four others who form the circle of poets that includes Horace, Ovid, Lucan and Homer. Though consigned to this first circle of Hell, through no fault of their own, Dante uses these figures of classic poetic authority to elevate himself in poetic stature:

> After they had talked awhile together, they turned to me with sign of salutation, at which my master smiled; and far more honor still they showed me, for they made me one of their company, so that I was sixth amid so much wisdom. (*Inf.* 4.97–102)

Along with the circle of poets, Dante provides a catalog of great philosophers, Avicenna, Galen, and Averroes among them, as well as other exemplary individuals, who suffer the same fate for lack of a Christian baptism. Limbo raises two important issues to be seen in other sections of *The Divine Comedy*. First, Virgil is his Master poet and Dante becomes a fellow in this group of model poets. Thus Dante's poetry is fitting for his lofty mission. Second, in terms of salvation, only Christians need apply. Perhaps since *The Divine Comedy* is fundamentally Dante's poem of conversion, he relegates these distinguished Muslim scholars to Limbo since they were responsible for informing much of the intellectual community of Dante's time.[7]

Leaving the heathens in the 1st circle, Virgil brings Dante to the edge of Hell Proper—circles 2 through 9—that is guarded by Minos, one of the many monsters found in Hell.[8] Dante further divides the canticle structurally. Hell Proper consists of two areas: Upper Hell, spanning circles 2 through 5, deals with sins of incontinence, while Lower Hell, also called the City of Dis, ranges from circles 6 through 9 and deals with sins of malice.[9] In Upper Hell, each group of incontinents, those guilty of sins of lust, gluttony, avarice, and wrath, are guarded or managed by monsters.

One of the most commented episodes of the *Inferno* occurs in Upper Hell. As Dante proceeds under the guidance of Virgil, his senses are assaulted by gruesome images of punishment. In an area of the 2nd circle that is bashed and battered by crushing winds, Dante finds Francesca and Paolo, two lovers recognizable to both the poet and his readers. When he asks Francesca how Love could possibly have brought them to such a tormented place, she explains:

There is no greater sorrow than to recall, in wretchedness, the happy time ... One day, for pastime, we read of Lancelot, how love constrained him; we were alone, suspecting nothing. Several times that reading urged our eyes to meet ... When we read how the longed-for smile was kissed by so great a lover, this one, who never shall be parted from me, kissed my mouth all trembling. A Gallehault was the book and he who wrote it; that day we read no farther in it. (*Inf.* 5.121–138)

The scene is truly rich, merely judging the episode on its literary intertextuality. The reference to Lancelot calls to mind the Arthurian legends that had circulated widely by Dante's time. The mention of Gallehault (Galeotto) is most appropriate as he was go-between for Lancelot's meetings with Guinevere. The strength of the scene far exceeds two literary references. Singleton pointed out in his commentary on the passage that "suspecting nothing" ("sanza alcun sospetto") can provoke several readings, but he preferred the sense of not suspecting the full force of their yet undeclared love for each other to that of having no witnesses, such that their aloneness ("soli eravamo") produces more tension as the reading of the Galeotto then provokes much more Love and consequently greater sin.

Dante does not leave the scene there, however. He closes the canto with: "While the one spirit said this, the other wept, so that for pity I swooned, as if in death, and fell as a dead body falls." (*Inf.* 5.139–142) So just as Francesca and Paolo interrupted their reading with a kiss, Dante here falls in a faint, disrupting the scene for his readers. His faint draws the attention of his readers away from the sin. The reaction of Dante-pilgrim is appropriate to the misery of the two lovers and realistic in the mind of the audience Dante-poet has targeted. The winds that torment the lovers in this circle are fitting allegorical representations of the tossing back and forth that Love's addictions can provoke. Similarly, Love's excesses as related in the romances of which the story of Lancelot is exemplary are paralleled to the obsessive rhetoric that this genre employed.

Just as Virgil must use "fair speech" to foster Dante's deliverance, the Poet engages his audience with allegorical disruptions and effective language. As Dante and Virgil make their way from one circle to another, Dante-poet calls attention to his use of the vernacular. In *Inf.*16

Dante-pilgrim hears three Florentines, in *Inf.* 26, Dante grieves that Florence is so well represented in Hell, and in *Inf.* 24.76, a sinner recognizes Dante by his Tuscan speech ("parola tosca").

If in *The Divine Comedy* Dante uses the vernacular and other linguistic playfulness to capture his audience, in his *De vulgare eloquentia*, (*The eloquence of the vernacular*) Dante accomplished two other goals. Dante explained language as a concept and provided a history of the linguistic changes he imagined emanating from the Garden of Eden through Babel to his own Italy. In the work that he began about 1302 after his exile from Florence and abandoned some years later, Dante praises "the language of people who speak the vulgar tongue" over that of the "grammatica," that artificial and rule-based language only acquired through years of study. A work that is still categorized among Dante's *opere minori*, the *De vulgare* has received more deserving attention especially in the later half of the 20th century. The treatise consists of a total of 23 chapters in two books. While the second book's focus is narrower and covers aspects of poetic composition, the first book bears on *The Divine Comedy*, and in particular the sections of the *Inferno* where Dante makes note of the language in use. In the *De vulgare*'s first book, Dante describes the linguistic variations of the peoples of "oc, oïl, sì," roughly matching Provence, northern France, and Italy, and in turn points out the one factor that links them and their linguistic development. They speak different languages because they are sinners. The expulsion from the Garden of Eden and the architecture of Babel underscore the fact that these peoples speak the language of their ancestors who were sinners, too. So in terms of the *Inferno*, Dante uses language as a conduit of recognition, of other sinners as well as of sin itself. The decay that takes place in death and in the suffering that is Hell also must take place as language develops. Just as Dante-pilgrim searches for the right way away from sin, Dante, author of the *De vulgare*, seeks a "vulgare illustre" having the power to transform the ways humans express themselves and their lives. In terms of the critical debate over allegory and realism, then, Dante's work is allegory, like the word's etymological definition suggests, since it deals with "other speaking." Its reality is Dante's use of vernacular traditions such as Old French romances and Provençal and Sicilian lyric, an intertextuality that in the hands of Dante follows his self-imposed rule of fitting the situation or mission.

The power of language is manifest in Lower Hell. In the City of Dis, four different degrees of malice are punished in circles 6 through 9: the heretics, the violent, the fraudulent, and finally the traitors. Each circle has sub-divisions of differing numbers, usually following Dante's preferred numbers of 3, 4, and 10. In the 9th circle there are four areas where traitors to family, country, guests, and lords suffer unimaginable pain. In the first ring, called Caina, Dante uses language once again as a signpost of identification as the sinner gnawing the head of another says to him: "I do not know who you are … but truly you seem to me Florentine when I hear you." (*Inf.* 33.10–12)

The speaker is Count Ugolino, a historical figure recognizable to Dante's audience as a participant in the Guelph-Ghilbelline conflict, the same political crisis that provoked Dante's exile. Ugolino, a Guelph, was imprisoned with his sons and grandsons. In this most desperate scene, Dante-pilgrim witnesses with revulsion as Ugolino's teeth penetrate the skull of Archbishop Ruggieri, the Ghibelline responsible for the deaths by starvation of Ugolino and his family. The opening horror is not gratuitous. If the reader observes Ugolino devouring Ruggieri "as bread is devoured by hunger" (*Inf.* 32.127), learns of his dream of sharp-fanged dogs and sees him bite his own hand, then the reader has full knowledge of the barbarity of which Ugolino is capable. As Ugolino relates to Dante the terror of being sealed up in the prison with his male progeny, the implication of his words intensifies:

> And below I heard them nailing up the door of the horrible tower; whereat I looked in the faces of my children without a word. I did not weep, so was I turned to stone within me. (*Inf.* 33.46–49)

The distress of realizing his children's fate strips Ugolino of language. At the same time, Dante-poet makes use of familiar, childlike language when little Anselm asks what ails his dad ("Tu guardi sì, padre! Che hai?" *Inf.* 33.51). And it is the suggestion of his children that their father eat them when Dante's language of ambiguity produces the greatest revulsion: "Then fasting did more than grief had done." (*Inf.* 33.75) Of the many readings put forth in Dante scholarship, suggesting that indeed Ugolino practiced cannibalism or that the scene evoked the sacrifice of the Eucharist, the most compelling assertion comes from Jorge Luis Borges. In one of his *Nine Dantesque Essays*, Borges believes that the power of the Ugolino's unspeakable act is the very suggestion of its possibility: "Dante did not want us to believe it, but he wanted us to suspect it." (Borges, 278)

Still reeling from this ghastly scene, the pilgrim and his readers must descend to the lowest point of Hell to see Lucifer devouring the three greatest traitors, Judas Iscariot, Brutus, and Cassius. Only then do Dante and Virgil climb the stairs leading out of Lucifer's lair. Next, in the second book of *The Divine Comedy*, Dante describes Purgatory, which he envisioned as a steep mountain, on the opposite side of the Earth from Jerusalem. The deepness of Hell is replaced by the steepness of the mountain as the sinners work their way upwards to Paradise and God. And in a reversed topological order to that of Hell, the sins being purged decrease in severity as Dante-pilgrim and Virgil ascend.

Once again, the idea of *contrapasso* supports the organization of Purgatory. The location and suffering of each sinner are appropriate to the individual's sinful disposition. Here too there are spatial divisions within Purgatory. Of the three present, the first is Ante-Purgatory where the inhabitants still feel atmospheric changes from Earth. These sinners postponed the cleansing of their sins on earth and now must wait at the foot of the mountain. In the second area, Purgatory proper, there are seven terraces corresponding to the seven capital sins. Instead of monsters guarding each level as in Hell, angels watch over the entrances to the terraces. The third division is called Earthly Paradise and is found at the top of the mountain.

Passages, from one area to another, are marked quite dramatically throughout the poem. Here in Purgatory, as well, the passage from Ante-Purgatory into Purgatory proper through a gate receives due consideration. The Poet calls to his readers: "You see well, reader, that I uplift my theme: do not wonder, therefore, if I sustain it with greater art." (*Purg.* 9.70–72) Not only does Dante use the verb "see" as he does repeatedly in the opening of the *Purgatorio*, he also elevates the material just as the mountain's steepness increases. The reader, like the pilgrim, is about to experience loftier challenges, consequently the need for higher art. Still Virgil must reassure the pilgrim as he approaches the three steps, colored white, purple, and red, and the intense gaze of the angelic gatekeeper. Spatial symmetries contrast Hell and Purgatory just as the vice guarded by monsters in Hell also markedly differs from the virtue of God's angels. Contrasting the warning of Minos, the monster guarding the 2nd circle of Hell, this gatekeeper is an angel who places seven *P—P* for *peccatum*, sin—on the pilgrim's forehead and admonishes him: "See that you wash away these wounds when you are within." (*Purg.* 9.113–114) The pilgrim feels changed, both by Virgil's reassuring words and the angel's counsel. After all, Dante-pilgrim is now in Purgatory where pain purifies sins and where remediation and redemption are the ultimate goal.

The seven *P*, one for each of the cardinal sins, also weigh down the pilgrim. Dante uses these to organize his loftier material in Purgatory. The sins of pride, envy and wrath are purged in the first three terraces. Souls cleansing sins of sloth are punished on the 4th terrace. Those of excessive love—avarice, gluttony, and lust—expunge their sins on the highest three terraces. On the way up from the first to the second terrace, an angel approaches the pilgrim. The "fair creature" removes one *P* from Dante's forehead, recites from the beatitudes and shows the travelers the passage to the next terrace. The scene repeats itself at each terrace thus showing another organizational device inserted by Dante fitting both structure and content. At this juncture, Dante turns to Virgil and remarks: "Master, tell me, what weight has been lifted from me that I feel almost no weariness as I go on?" (*Purg.* 12.118–120) Virgil explains that the sharpness of the ascent and the narrowness of the way will soon offer no challenge to the Pilgrim as he progressively frees himself from the burden of each sin.

As the two climb their way through Purgatory, Dante-poet emphasizes three sins in particular by having his pilgrim self share the suffering of those he sees. Dante-pilgrim stoops down to speak with the prideful souls on the first terrace who are burdened by the heavy weight of their sin; on the third, the pilgrim must deal with the smoke blinding those purging the sin of anger; and finally, on the seventh terrace, Dante passes through the lust-purging fire, but only after Virgil resorts to naming Beatrice to persuade him to face the fire's torment.

If some have suggested that these three sins and the pilgrim's participation at some level in their purging reflects an autobiographical note in the poem, surely the inclusion of poets throughout the poem and Dante's citation of his own poetic tradition bring out the man in the work. Though it is troubling to find exemplary poets such as Bertran de Born in Hell,[10] Dante elevates himself to the masterful level of the circle of classic poets in Limbo and in the *Purgatorio* he includes himself and other poets in his material of higher art. Casella the singer moves to embrace Dante three times (*Purg.* 2), evoking the scene from Virgil's

Aeneid in which Aeneas meets his father in the afterworld. Dante is unsure at first, and then finally recognizes Casella by his voice. When Dante requests that Casella comfort his weariness, Casella sings "Love that discourses in my mind" ("Amor che ne la mente me ragiona"), the opening verse of *canzone* 2 from Dante's *Convivio*. The citation of his own work becomes part of Casella's sweet song such that: "My master and I and that folk who were with him appeared content as if naught else touched the mind of any." Both the living and the dead then receive comfort from Dante's cited words in a scene poetically linked to one written by Virgil years earlier.[11]

Virgil connects the encounter with the next poet, seen resting not far from the gate of Purgatory. It is Sordello, another Mantuan and a great Italian poet known for writing in Provençal. The meeting of the two Mantuan poets offers Dante the opportunity for Virgil to explain his residence in Limbo:

> A place there is below, not sad with torments but with darkness only, where the lamentations sound not as wailings, but are sighs. There I abide with the little innocents, seized by the fangs of death before they were exempted from human guilt; there I abide with those who were not clothed with the three holy virtues ... (*Purg.* 7.28–35)

The three virtues—faith, hope, and charity—are the result of baptism and without these an individual would be incapable of meriting salvation. Dante-poet has his pagan Master articulate Christian beliefs regarding baptism and salvation. Yet despite the fact that Virgil is Beatrice's instrument used for the pilgrim's deliverance from sin, Virgil will nevertheless remain in Limbo.

Sordello, in turn, serves to contrast the appearance of another poet. Virgil and Dante recognize Statius on the fifth terrace. While Virgil explains Limbo to Sordello, Statius bows before Virgil and tells him of the inspiration gained from his poems, which made Statius understand the errors of his wastefulness and excess. Empowered by Virgil's words (*Purg.* 22.73), Statius embraced Christianity and will be a poet who eventually enters Paradise. Statius the converted pagan then accompanies Dante further on the journey than Virgil the unbaptized. He must leave the two as they enter the Earthly Paradise, the tenth level of Purgatory, where souls wait to enter into blessedness.

On the sixth terrace where sins of gluttony are purged, Dante uses poet Bonagiunta da Lucca to cite another passage from his own work. The line "Ladies that have intelligence of love" ("Donna ch'avete intelletto d'amore") is from the *Vita Nuova* 19. Dante does not use the insertion to speak of his songbook dedicated to Love. Rather, it allows Bonagiunta to name himself and his two contemporaries, Giacomo da Lentini and Guittone d'Arezzo, as those held back by Dante's "sweet new style" ("dolce stil nuovo" *Purg.* 24.57). Dante discusses his own lyric style set within the context of earlier poetic production. Through Bonagiunta's words, Dante expresses his belief that he has succeeded where the earlier poets failed in synthesizing style and subject matter. Commentaries, especially those from the 19th century, read this passage as Dante's intention to found a "new school" of poetics rather than Dante proposing a fellowship with his contemporaries. The circle including Guinizzelli, Cavalcanti, Cino da Pistoia, and Dante fostered a new lyric tradition that was characterized as sweet or pleasing to the ear where Love is both intellectually and spiritually ennobling. Fitting Dante's purposes and borne out by her role in *The Divine Comedy*, Beatrice manifests Dante's personal poetic evolution since her character begins as the object of his earthly Love in the *Vita Nuova*, but acts in the *Paradiso* as the catalyst for Dante-pilgrim to learn about an intellectually based Love with spiritual dimensions.

On the very next terrace, where sins of lust are punished, Dante encounters two other poets who provide yet another opportunity for him to promote his own poetics. One is Guinizzelli, just cited by reference to the "dolce stil nuovo." Though reverentially called "il saggio" in the *Vita Nuova* (20.3), here Dante's words, this time in the mouth of Cavalcanti, suggest that it is Dante who has surpassed earlier lyric tradition when Cavalcanti says that even Lethe, the river of oblivion cannot erase the traces left by Dante's style (*Purg.* 26.106-108). Guinizzelli points out Arnaut Daniel, the second poet on this terrace, as a "better craftsman of the mother tongue." Arnaut speaks to Dante in Provençal, the language he so championed in his poetry, paralleling the encounter between Sordello, an Italian who preferred Provençal in his poetry, and Virgil who wrote in Latin. Dante's praise for Arnaut is undeniable here, yet by calling him "craftsman" ("fabbro") rather than "poet" the passage further insinuates that Dante's pride was not completely cleansed when leaving the first terrace. Unlike Dante both

Cavalcanti and Arnaut pass through the fires purging sinners of lust with ease and noted haste since they have corrected their faults.

And it is a poet that sends Dante on to his ultimate goal. Virgil, the master poet, bids farewell to Dante as the pilgrim prepares for the most crucial of passages, that into the Divine Presence. It is fitting then that Virgil stress in his last speech to Dante that the pilgrim must—with his will, free and whole—become his own guide. Throughout the *Inferno* but especially in the *Purgatorio*, Dante has underscored the fate of the sinners as a true and good consequence of their will. His appointed guide Virgil can go no further but urges Dante on, again with difficulty. Only at the mention of Beatrice's name does Dante willfully shift his fears long enough to jump through the flames separating the seventh terrace of Purgatory from Earthly Paradise. There, Beatrice will appear for the first time. The passage that she initiates, full of pageantry and charged with numerological significance, marks Dante's most emotional outburst in his journey. His former Love confronts and rebukes him; her direct attack is so thorough that Beatrice brings Dante to confess his guilt, thus preparing the way for him to pass, temporarily at least, into Paradise.

Dante structured the third and final canticle, the *Paradiso*, on the basis of the Ptolomeic system, which imagined nine concentric heavens revolving around the Earth and a tenth heaven, the Empyrean, beyond time and space and therefore motionless. According to this system, the Empyrean is where redeemed souls sit, arranged in a white celestial rose, some closer to God than others. *Contrapasso* in its definition of describing punishment suited to the offense does not strictly apply in the arrangement of Paradise. Its sense of appropriateness does, though, since merit determines nearness to God. The souls who have reached Paradise have done so because of their exemplary behavior on Earth. Just as the sinners in Hell and Purgatory, so too those enjoying heavenly bliss are fittingly noted according to their earthly dispositions. And as in the *Inferno* and the *Purgatorio*, the variety of punishments there is balanced in the *Paradiso* by the diversity of happiness experienced by the redeemed souls. The multiplicity of bliss as envisioned by Dante echoes the beliefs of St. Augustine and St. Thomas Aquinas in proposing that individuals differ in their capacity for loving God. Though Dante does not provide detailed reasons for the souls' ultimate locations in the *Paradiso*, each one descends from the celestial rose to meet the pilgrim on a revolving heaven suitable to the soul's Earthly life.

Each meeting is an opportunity for speech, explanation, and debate. Each contributes to Dante's preparation for entering the Divine Presence. Though truly the entire trajectory through Hell and Purgatory is part of his training, the first thirty cantos focus on the cleansing of his intellect and the strengthening of his spirit. Beatrice, the perfect escort, exacts close attention from Dante as they proceed through the nine concentric heavens. She is guide, teacher, judge, and most notably, theologian. Through the words of Beatrice, and the other souls he meets along the way, Dante can espouse the Christian beliefs he held so dearly. Where in the *Inferno* the tortured sinners deserve their gruesome justice and in the *Purgatorio* Dante conversed with poets to show how poetry cleanses and elevates, here in the *Paradiso* the action of speech expands the intellectual and spiritual essence of the pilgrim. Yet this should not imply that all speech is directed, via Beatrice's guidance, to a theological end.

Cacciaguida, for example, greets Dante on Mars; the fifth sphere of celestial intelligence that influences human courage and is linked to the Roman god of war. Cacciaguida is one of many speakers that Dante encounters in Paradise. His message spans three cantos and relates to war, faith, and the future. He is Dante's great-great-grandfather and celebrates his Christian faith and his participation in the Crusades

> ... against the iniquity of that law whose people, through fault
> of the Pastors, usurp your rights. There by that foul folk was
> I released from the deceitful world, the love of which debases
> many souls, and I came from martyrdom to this peace. (*Par.*
> 15.142–148)

His death as a martyr in the Christian holy war is not the only matter for discussion at hand. Cacciaguida in *Par.* 16 provides an extensive history lesson replete with Homeric catalogs of ancestral names and localities used to describe family heritage and the glory that once was Florence. The canto evokes two of Dante's earlier works, yet not in the direct way he inserts verses from his past poems in other parts of *The Divine Comedy*. Cacciaguida's stories of Florentine growth and decline echo political theories put forth in the *Monarchia*, Dante's treatise on government written during his exile, while the discourse on noble families is reminiscent of Dante's fourth book of the *Convivio* where he proposes that nobility emanates from moral worth and not ancestral wealth.

When Cacciaguida speaks of the future, his words lament the decline of Florence and imply the inevitable exile Dante will suffer. He reassures Dante that with the help of another born under the influence of Mars, Can Grande della Scala, he and others will have their fortunes altered. He charges Dante to write despite the obstacles:

> A conscience dark, either with its own or with another's shame, will indeed feel your speech to be harsh. But none the less, all falsehood aside, make manifest all that you have seen; and then let them scratch where the itch is. (*Par.* 17.124–126)

The dark, like the dark wood where the lost Dante began his journey, suggests the dismal times ahead for Dante when, during exile, he will be adrift and far from his beloved Florence. The passage also implies that Dante's mission is personal as well as divinely inspired. Further, it calls attention to the language Dante will use and conveys Dante's overarching attitude of bringing his quest closer to his readers.

Another noble speaker appears in the second sphere, Mercury. It is Justinian, the codifier of Roman law, whose speech recounts the evolution of the Empire from Aeneas landing in Italy through Romulus, Hannibal, Scipio, Julius Caesar, to Tiberius and finally the birth and crucifixion of Christ whose church Charlemagne protected as the Holy Roman Emperor. Like the address delivered by Cacciaguida, Justinian's message links history to Dante's lot in life. He is an Emperor who lectures Dante on the long trajectory of ambitious men and events, which produced the political world in which Dante lives. Justinian links the past to the Guelph-Ghibelline conflict while his words allows Dante to praise the authority of the empire, as he did in the *Monarchia*, his treatise on the empire and the papacy. The three books comprising the *Monarchia* completed in the last years of his life contend that in the world order as envisioned by Dante one single emperor is best since this system provides unity to mankind. His intellectual impetus is visibly Agustinian as seen in Dante's use of concepts put forth in the *City of God*. Dante's message in the treatise is fundamentally Christian. The sole emperor must work in close harmony with the pope in order to temper his governing with spiritual guidance, suggesting that by this time of his

life Dante had at least intellectually reconciled a balance between the
papist and imperialist forces characteristic of the Guelph-Ghibelline
struggle.

Though Dante deals here with ancestry, nobility, politics, and
other personal interests, the bulk of the *Paradiso* is a theological and
philosophical *discursus* managed by Beatrice throughout the thirty-three
cantos. Beatrice brings Dante before St. Peter for an examination of his
faith. She leads him to St. James who questions him on hope, as does St.
John on charity. It is Beatrice who not only directs his oral examinations
but also requires that Dante heed her lessons for his spiritual edification.
But finally, the once silent object of his love chronicled in the *Vita Nuova*
now speaks.

When, in *Vita Nuova* 14, Dante sees Beatrice among other female
wedding guests, he faints. His obsession to mask his love for her publicly
overwhelms him. In the opening of the *Inferno*, Dante once again finds
himself less than conscious, and Virgil, on Beatrice's beckoning, must
awaken him. Repeatedly in the *Inferno* and the *Purgatorio*, Virgil must
resort to naming Beatrice to persuade Dante to face the next challenge.
She continues her muted presence even as the resplendent pageant
announces her arrival at the end of the *Purgatorio*.

Beatrice vocalizes Dante's ideas. Her voice evolves from one used,
while still in the Earthly Paradise, to admonish and rebuke Dante's
errors and lost way. But in the full benefit of the powers ascribed to her
in Paradise, she not only has a voice but often it is on a par or exceeds
the masculine ones that so inform the philosophical and moral
foundation of his epic poem.

The love portrayed in the *Vita Nuova* follows the tradition
established by earlier romances and represents the love gone astray that
provokes the sins punished in Hell or expunged in Purgatory. This
songbook of love is Dante's earliest work and combines prose and poetry.
There are thirty-one lyric poems, mostly sonnets, whose style and
language link prior troubadour tradition with Dante's circle of poet-
friends writing in the "sweet new style." His little book also speaks of
poetry; first by its dedication to Guido Cavalcanti, and throughout the
work in the prose explanations Dante offers after each lyric. Yet more
far-reaching than its poetics, the *Vita Nuova* sets up Beatrice as the
motivation for *The Divine Comedy* and announces her superiority over all
other women:

... [T]here appeared to me a marvelous vision in which I saw things which made me decide to write no more of this blessed one until I could do so more worthily. And to this end I apply myself as much as I can, as she indeed knows. Thus, if it shall please Him by whom all things live that my life continue for a few years, I hope to compose concerning her what has never been written in rhyme of any women. (*Vita Nuova* 42.1–8)

Beatrice is heralded here as an integral part of Dante's divine mission in writing *The Divine Comedy*. Her superiority, not merely over other women, comes into play as Beatrice explains a constellation of ideas and teachings held by Church fathers and philosophical masters. In *Par.* 2.58*ff*, Beatrice conducts a scholastic exercise for Dante by putting a question to him, listening to and then correcting his answer. As Singleton explained in his commentary to the canto, Beatrice's explanation of the spots on the moon includes ideas promoted by Plato and Aristotle, and later dealt with by Augustine and Aquinas. The passage also echoes studies by Albertus Magnus and Averroes and ultimately shows Dante's preference for a spiritual rather than a material explanation for the phenomenon.

As mentioned already, Virgil often relies on Beatrice's name as a tool to bring Dante along on his arduous path to salvation; Virgil also admits to the limitations of reason and recommends that Dante rely on Beatrice's faith (*Purg.* 18.46-48) thus relinquishing his role as Master poet in deference to hers as interpreter of faith and truth. If Dante cites his own work within his epic poem, he does so to identify himself among the many other layers of authority presented in the work. By having Beatrice explain and often contradict learned teachings, Dante elevates her authority to a divine level, far exceeding traditionally masculine tenets held in philosophy and breaking the boundaries of muted feminine beauty.

Beatrice's physicality is not overlooked, though, in the *Paradiso*. Numerous references to her eyes and her smile fill the third canticle. Having just listened to Cacciaguida's sad prediction regarding his future, Dante finds consolation in Beatrice's beauty:

I turned round ... and what love I saw in the holy eyes I leave here untold; not only because I distrust my own speech, but

> because of memory, which cannot return on itself so far
> unless Another guide it. This much of that moment can I
> retell, that as I gazed upon her my affection was freed from
> every other desire so long as the Eternal Joy that shone direct
> on Beatrice satisfied me from the fair eyes with its reflected
> aspect. Overcoming me with the light of a smile, she said to
> me, "Turn and listen, for not only in my eyes is Paradise."
> (*Par.* 18.7–21)

Dante loses control of his greatest instrument, his speech, in her presence. His very memory, that crucial faculty of which the *Vita Nuova* is a celebration in Beatrice's name, becomes untrustworthy.

Her physical beauty comforts Dante often while simultaneously allowing him access to those in Paradise. When Charles Martel cites the opening line from the first *canzone* in Dante's *Convivio* ("Voi che 'ntendendo il terzo ciel movete" / "O Intelligences moving the third heaven"), Dante looks at Beatrice reverentially (*Par.* 8.40) as if to request permission to speak to Martell. This is the third time Dante has inserted his own verses in the poem. On this occasion as well as the others, the listener is openly pleased by Dante's words.

The *Convivio* brings to mind a possible rival to Beatrice, not a mere human female—though this too is implied—but Lady Philosophy, the inspiration of Boethius' *Consolation of Philosophy* and the allegorical motivation for many masterful essays in Dante's collection of earlier authorities. Dante uses Lady Philosophy to personify two ideals he held quite high: knowledge (*scienza*) and wisdom (*sapienza*). His treatise bears several similarities to that of Boethius. Both mix genres (prose and poetry). Both authors apologize for speaking of themselves in their own works. Dante wrote his work while in exile from Florence and Boethius composed his treatise while imprisoned for treachery. The most compelling element that the two texts share is the belief that knowledge is empowering, facilitating a liberation of the soul and bringing about happiness. Like *The Divine Comedy*, there is a mixture of the literal and the allegorical in the *Convivio*. Lady Philosophy is the perfect bride of God. She is both love and wisdom in one entity whose beauty ennobles and inspires much like Beatrice:

> Things in her aspect ever I detect,
> that show us ecstasies of Paradise—

I mean, in her sweet smile and in her eyes,
which Love left here as in their proper home.[12]
(*Convivio*, 2nd *canzone*, 55–58)

Unlike Boethius' object of inspiration, Dante's Lady Philosophy does not speak. And in stark contrast, Beatrice's gaze and smile quietly reinforce her powers of speech. No longer verbally mute, Beatrice's true realization as the underlying force and motivation of Dante's work reveals itself in her words. Not only is she Dante's resource for faith and truth and the interpreter of demanding philosophical thought, Beatrice functions in these roles "by my judgment, which cannot err." (*Par.* 7.19) In the Italian text, the word Beatrice uses to declare the full extent of her powers is "infallibile," a word heard in modern times associated only with the Pope when speaking on Church matters and in God's name. The conduit for expressing his knowledge and thought as poet-creator of the work in which she speaks, Beatrice is thus elevated to a divine level of authority which in turn advances Dante's voice in his text. Dante often states in the *Paradiso* that his language does not serve to describe Paradise. The series of speakers who appear in the heavenly spheres speak for Dante. The most eloquent is Beatrice who is able to voice wondrous thoughts until she departs, after bringing Dante into reach of the celestial rose.

The pilgrim has already been bathed and transformed by divine light—"I comprehended that I was surmounting beyond my own power" (*Par.* 30.56–57)—when Beatrice tells him he must drink from the waters of the river of light in order to approach the Divine Presence. This is Dante's final baptism and another opportunity for Dante to stress his Christian belief that the cleansing of sin permits entrance into the Empryean, the highest sphere of Paradise. At this point of transition, the reader is reminded of the last exchange of escorts. Virgil turned over the pilgrim to Beatrice. According to Dante's conservative Christian point of view, Virgil and others like Avicenna and Averroes, still hampered by original sin, must reside in Limbo. Statius the converted pagan poet accompanied Dante further on his journey than Virgil could. Here, at the point when Bernard of Clairvaux takes the place of Beatrice for the last part of the journey, Dante accentuates the transition made possible by the river's baptizing light.

Dante is momentarily surprised to see an old man where Beatrice once stood. Bernard points out the location to where Beatrice ascended.

Relieved, Dante sees Beatrice who smiles at him one last time as she turns to take her appointed place in the celestial rose. But Bernard wants Dante to focus at a higher point in the rose where a thousand angels surround the abbot's inspiration: Mary, the mother of God. Bernard then names many of those joined with Mary in God's presence. These blessed souls joined in a holy choir are heard singing Mary's praises as Bernard opens the final canto with his prayer in devotion to Mary. The pilgrim has survived a morally arduous personal struggle to arrive at his ultimate destiny, if only for a fleeting moment. The poet, lamenting his lack of speech and memory, feels inadequate as he attempts to recreate bliss in the poem he writes:

> ... for my sight, becoming pure, was entering more and more
> through the beam of the lofty Light which in Itself is true.
> Thenceforward my vision was greater than speech can show,
> which fails at such a sight, and at such excess memory fails.
> (*Inf.* 33.51–57)

The poet whose self-promoted treasure is his language and his verse finds himself incapable of expressing the vision that he believed himself divinely inspired to express. Singing and prayer usher in Dante's final song, which extols the divine love that "moves the sun and the other stars." (*Par.* 33.145) Dante's angle of vision once again turns upward from where the Poet sits looking to the heavens, just as he did at the beginning of his struggle to find the straight path out of the "dark wood" and again at the foot of Purgatory as he stared up its precipitous slopes. The final verse of the poem underscores Dante's understanding of his place in God's universe. Whether the compendium of scholarship we use today when approaching the text enlightens or exasperates, the work unfailingly leaves its reader looking upward.

NOTES

1. *terza rima*: "A verse form composed of iambic tercets rhyming aba, bcb, etc., the second line of the first tercet supplying the rhyme for the second tercet, the second line of the second tercet supplying the rhyme for the third, and so on, thus giving the effect of linkage to the entire composition." *Princeton Encyclopedia of Poetry and Poetics*. Alex Preminger, ed. (Princeton: Princeton University Press, 1965), 847–8.

2. *Inf.* 16.127–128 "per le note/de questa commedia, lettor, ti giuro" ("reader, I swear to you by the notes of this comedy") and *Inf.* 21.1–2 "altro parlando/che la mia commedìa cantar non cura" ("talking of things of which my comedy is not concerned to sing").

3. Curtius finds this awakening most significant: "The 'awakening' of Aristotle in the thirteenth century was the work of generations and took place in the cool light of intellectual research. The awakening of Virgil by Dante is an arc of flame which leaps from one great soul to another. The tradition of the European spirit knows no situation of such affecting loftiness, tenderness, fruitfulness. It is the meeting of the two greatest Latins." Curtius, *European Literature and the Latin Middle Ages*, 358.

4. In honoring Virgil's role as poet-model, Dante exclaims: "O glory and light of other poets, may the long study and the great love that have made me search your volume avail me! You are my master and my author. You alone are he from whom I took the fair style that has done me honor. " (*Inf.* 1.82–87)

5. Both the dating of the fictional journey and the fact that Dante writes of a time in his past have received a great deal of critical attention. First, by the astrological elements mentioned in the text, some critics have tried to pinpoint the actual time of the pilgrim's journey. Others have paid more attention to the allegorical value of journeying to redemption in relation to the Christian time of the resurrection.

The second element is more intriguing for the reader. Dante can play with recent, recognizable events to make his point. For example, he refers to Guelph and Ghibelline conflicts by mentioning those involved in the crisis that forced Dante into exile.

6. Once again Dante echoes many authorities in his sense of appropriateness. *Contrapasso* has Biblical roots in the law of retaliation (*lex talionis*) as seen in *Exodus* 21:23ff and *Leviticus* 24:17–20. It is also present in the New Testament in *Matthew* 5:38. In the classics, Virgil,

Seneca, and Aristotle treated similar ideas. Aquinas represents the Christian model, Dante's most often-cited source. The Islamic *Book of the Ladder of Muhammed* should also be considered here as a possible source.

7. Dante assigns Mohammed and Ali to Hell in the Malebolge ("evil pouches") as schismatics. (*Inf.* 28) See Menocal, 127.

8. Minos is the monster who assigns to each soul its place in Hell, not judgmentally—since all have chosen their lot by their own will—but administratively. Cerberus, Plutus, and Phlegyas are the other monsters, this last one being the ferryman of the Styx.

9. Dante follows Aristotle's theories on the division of sin as found in the *Nichomachean Ethics*. But while Aristotle identifies 3 types—malice, incontinence, and bestiality—Dante prefers to treat fraud as his third type of sin, thus echoing Cicero's theories on force and fraud. Once again, Dante takes classical models and makes them his own, in this work in particular by adding typically Christian ideas.

10. For an insightful commentary on the presence of Bertran de Born in the same location as Mohammed in the circle of Hell punishing schismatics, see Mazzotta's *Dante's Vision*, 92–95.

11. See Barolini, *Dante's Poets*, especially her chapter on auto-citation.

12. Translation from Tusiani, 77.

JAMES MERRILL

Divine Poem

Many readers will have encountered, as I did, their first Dante in the "Prufrock" epigraph. We learned to smile at the juxtaposition of ineffectual daydreamer and damned soul speaking from the fire. "For this is hell, nor are we out of it," we innocently marveled, peering forth from our own gemlike flames at worktable and bookshelf, sunset and dozing cat. Purgatory and paradise awaited us too, in the guise of the next love affair. In a single elegant stroke Eliot had shown us one way to approach *l'altissimo poeta*: Dante's passionate faith and our intrepid doubts could be reconciled by triangulation with the text itself.

To believe, however, that Dante had in any real sense seen God threatened both the poem and us. Who wanted song to curdle overnight into mere scripture, or himself to be trivialized in the glare of too much truth? Yet we must—or so I begin to think, decades later—allow that something distinct from mere "inspiration" came to Dante. It had come to others; he is not after all our only mystic, just more literary and more fortunate than many. In an age that discouraged the heretic, his vision reached him through the highest, most unexceptionable channels. Its cast included saints, philosophers, emperors, angels, monsters, Adam and Ulysses, Satan and God. To these he added a poet he revered, a woman he adored, plus a host of friends and enemies whose names we should otherwise never have heard; and garbed them in patterns of breathtakingly symmetrical lights-and-darks woven from a belief everybody shared. Even the pre-Christian souls in hell know pretty

From *The Poets' Dante* eds. Peter S. Hawkins and Rachel Jacoff (Farrar, Straus and Giroux, 2001). © 2001 by Peter S. Hawkins and Rachel Jacoff. Reprinted by permission of Farrar, Straus, and Giroux.

much what they are damned for not having known in time. No question
ever of an arcane, Blakean anti-mythology, Dante's conceptual innovations—as when he lifts purgatory to the surface of the earth, or
reveals his lady as an agent from highest heaven—refigure rather than
refute the thought that preceded them. As for his verbal ones, he was in
the historical position to consolidate, virtually to invent, for purposes
beyond those of the lyric, a living Italian idiom. No poet could ask for
more; yet more was given him.

Revelation can take many forms. St. Paul was "caught up into
paradise, and heard unspeakable words"—a one-shot trip. Milton, on the
other hand, dreamed each night the next day's installment of his poem.
Blake kept open house, through much of his life, for spirits with whom
he conversed wide awake. Yeats, married to a medium, took down the
voices that spoke through her. A lay visionary—where poetry is at issue,
someone whose powers of language and allusion aren't up to the
demands made upon them—reports a complex, joyous wonder
compressed into a few poor human moments and verging dangerously
upon the unutterable. Much as it may change his life, the experience
defeats his telling of it. Dante imagined this to be his case; it was not.

For he was already a poet. He had completed his apprenticeship in
lyrics of high perfection. As for allusion, he had read widely and seriously
if, to us, eccentrically. Homer lay beyond his ken, but he knew Paulus
Orosius and the *Voyage of St. Brendan*, and may well have come across
this sentence from the Sufi Ibn Arabi (found by me heading the chapter
on Beatrice in Irma Brandeis, *The Ladder of Vision*): "When she kills with
her glances, her speech restores to life as though she, in giving life, were
thereby Jesus."

The *Comedy's* energy and splendor suggest that Dante indeed "saw
the light" in a timeless moment. Its prophetic spleen and resonant
particulars hint at something not quite the same, that like Milton or
Yeats he had mediumistic powers—a sustaining divinatory intelligence
which spoke to him, if only (as Julian Jaynes would have it) from that
center of the brain's right hemisphere which corresponds to Weinecke's
area on the left. This much granted, it would still remain to be amazed
in the usual fashion when faced by a masterpiece: How on earth was it
brought safely into being and onto the page?

Poets nowadays are praised for performing without a net. "These
poems take risks!" gloat the blurbs. Akhmatova saddles Dante with a
cold and implacable Muse. I wonder. One does not wince *for* him the
way one does for Rimbaud. He is spared even the mortification of a

system that dates. The electronic marvels of paradise—stars clustering into eagles, and all that—have according to Beatrice been devised to suit the seer: a laser show of supreme illusion projected through Dante's human senses and image banks. (Do hell and purgatory keep being modernized to extract the maximum pain and penance from the new arrival? I suppose they do.) Page after page the Powers overwhelm the pilgrim, while treating the poet—the textures of his verse affirm it— with kid gloves.

A reader whose experience of *terza rima* is limited to Shelley can but faintly imagine its force and variety in the hands of its inventor. At the humblest level it serves as a No Trespassing sign, protecting the text. A copyist's pious interpolation or unthinking lapse would at once set off the alarm. No verse form *moves* so wonderfully. Each tercet's first and third line rhyme with the middle one of the preceding set and enclose the new rhyme-sound of the next, the way a scull outstrips the twin, already dissolving oar-strokes that propel it. As rhymes interlock throughout a canto, so do incidents and images throughout the poem. Thus any given tercet reflects in microcosm the triple structures explored by the whole, and the progress of the verse, which allows for closure only when (and because) a canto ends, becomes a version "without tears" of the pilgrim's own. Rendering here some lightning insight or action, there some laborious downward or upward clambering, the *terza rima* can as well sweeten the pill of dogmatic longueurs ("This keeps moving, it will therefore end") and frame with aching fleetness those glimpses of earth denied now to the damned and the blest alike.

We feel everywhere Dante's great concision. He has so *much* to tell. Self-limited to these bare hundred cantos averaging a scant 140 lines apiece, he can't afford to pad—he is likelier to break off, pleading no more room—let alone spell out connections for a torpid reader. This *we* must do, helped by centuries of commentary. And what a shock it is, opening the *Comedy*, to leave today's plush avant-garde screening room with its risk-laden images and scrambled sound track and use our muscles to actually get somewhere. For Dante's other great virtue is his matter-of-factness. Zodiacal signposts, "humble" similes, glosses from philosophy and myth—there is nothing he won't use to locate and focus his action as sharply as possible.

A random example. Sun is climbing toward noon above the Ganges as we enter a smoke "dark as night" on the slopes of purgatory;

meanwhile, these moles that come and go in a passing phrase are kin, surely, to Miss Moore's real toads:

> Ricorditi, lettor, se mai ne l'alpe
>   ti colse nebbia per la qual vedesti
>   non altrimenti che per pelle talpe …

Singleton renders this: "Recall, reader, if ever in the mountains a mist has caught you, through which you could not see except as moles do through skin…" Helpful; but was the mole in Dante's day thought to see through its *skin*? A note explains what is made clear enough in Longfellow's version, where alliteration, moreover, brings a certain music to "pelle talpe," that tiny consonantal lozenge we have paused, I trust, to savor:

> Remember, Reader, if e'er in the Alps
>   A mist o'ertook thee, through which thou couldst see
>   Not otherwise than through its membrane mole …

It is the merest instance of that matter-of-fact concision I have in mind, and makes a small plea for translation into verse such as this which deftly evokes, as prose or indeed rhymed versions so rarely can, the diction and emphasis of the original. (Why, oh, why is the Longfellow *Comedy* not in print? Comparing it with the latest prose version, by Charles Singleton, and allowing for pains rightly taken by the latter to *sound* like prose, one is struck by how often he has had apparently no choice but to hit on that good gray poet's very phrase. There is also Longfellow's delectable nineteenth-century apparatus, including essays by Ruskin and Lamartine—"Dante a fait la gazette florentine de la postérité"; Boccaccio's account of the dead Dante guiding his son to the missing final cantos of the *Paradiso*; and James Russell Lowell on the poet's monument in Ravenna: "It is a little shrine covered with a dome, not unlike the tomb of a Mohammedan saint… The *valet de place* says that Dante is not buried under it, but beneath the pavement of the street in front of it, where also, he says, he saw my Lord Byron kneel and weep.")

Those moles, to resume, are just one filament in a web whose circumference is everywhere. They presently mesh with an apostrophe to the imagination, which also sees without using its eyes. A case made in passing for divine inspiration ("A light moves you which takes form in heaven, of itself...") gives way to three trance-like visions—Procne, Haman, Amata—appropriate to this level of the mountain Dante climbs. The center of the web is still far off, almost half the poem away, but we may as well glance at it now.

The passage in question, long a commentators' favorite, has lately begun to engage the scientists as well. Mark A. Peterson proposes (*American Journal of Physics*, Dec. 1979) that Dante's universe "is not as simple geometrically as it at first appears, but actually seems to be a so-called 'closed' universe, the 3-sphere, a universe which also emerges as a cosmological solution of Einstein's equations in general relativity theory." Let who can, experience for themselves the full complexity and symmetry of the resulting figure. Roughly, two spheres are joined *at every point* through their "equator," itself a third sphere of sheer connectivity, and the whole suspended within a fourth dimension. The figure has finite volume but no boundary: "every point is interior."

On the threshold of the Empyrean, Dante is given his first glimpse of God, an infinitesimally small, intensely brilliant point reflected, before he turns to gaze at it directly, in Beatrice's eyes. Around it spin concentric rings or haloes gaining in brightness and speed in proportion to their closeness to it. These represent the angelic orders, from inmost seraphim to furthest messengers, and compose one of the two interconnected "semi-universes" of Peterson's figure. The other, also composed of nine rings, has at its center the little "threshing-floor" of earth far down at which Dante has just been peering, and extends through the geocentric levels to his present vantage in the Primum Mobile. What he is looking at now, explains Beatrice, is the "point" on which "the heavens and all nature are dependent." All nature: the mole and the mountain, the sinner and the sun.

That her words paraphrase Aquinas in a commentary on Aristotle cannot account for the hallucinatory wonder of this little point. We may picture it partly as a model of electrons whirling round the atomic nucleus—in our day, the point on which all nature and its destruction depend; partly as an abstracted solar system—only with the relative planetary speeds reversed, since these Intelligences turn physics inside out. According to Peterson, however, this is exactly what they do not do. For the fourth dimension here is speed of rotation, or in Dante's view the dimension of divine precedence. The inmost ring moves fastest, as does the Primum Mobile outermost among the other set, because both are nearest to God. The two universes, heavenly and natural; are alike governed by that tiny point. The vision as reported sets the mind reeling. What must it have been to experience?

Here too we understand, not for the first time, how Dante is helped by Beatrice. Seeing this light through her eyes will enable him to put it into words, to translate into his poem's measures those that depend upon this timeless and dimensionless point, to receive what he may of the mystery and not be struck mad or dumb by it. A further, more profound glimpse will indeed be largely wiped from his mind by the uncanny image of the Argo's shadow passing over amazed Neptune.

Concise and exact, Dante is naturally partial to points. We have come across others before this one: the "point" in the tale at which Paolo and Francesca read no further; the high "point" of the sun's meridian over Jerusalem; the "point" where all times are present, into which Cacciaguida gazes to read Dante's future. A children's book comes to mind—"Adventures of a Hole" or whatever—where the small round "hero" piercing the volume from front to back serves as focus to the picture on every page. It would be in some such fashion that each episode or passing image in Dante connects with absolute Good—or Evil. For there is finally the very terrible point in the last canto of the *Inferno*. At the moral and physical universes' nether pole, it is the other center required by Peterson's scheme.

Here also are angelic spheres, those of the fallen angels, Satan, who as Lucifer belonged to that halo nearest the point of light, now towers waist-deep in ice, "constrained by all the weights of the universe," and at first glance oddly unthreatening. Nine rings narrow downward to this figure of raging entropy. From one to the next we have felt the movement decelerating. Wind-driven souls (Francesca) give way to runners (Brunetto), to the painfully walking hypocrites cloaked in gilded lead, to the frozen, impacted souls Cocytus. This is "natural" movement; unlike those angels of the Empyrean, it obeys the second law of thermodynamics. W. D. Snodgrass has traced (*In Radical Pursuit*) the pilgrim Dante's regression, as he faces the murderers of parents and children, through the traumatic phases of early childhood, infancy, and birth. Last comes this nadir, this "point" he must pass in order to be reborn. It lies at the exact center of earth, of gravity, of the entire Ptolemaic universe. As the pilgrims skirt it, everything abruptly turns upside down, psychological time once again flows forward, and their ascent begins toward the starlight of earth's further side.

To my knowledge no one appears to have defined this point much beyond the account of it above. "Here all is dark, and mysterious," says Singleton. Dante himself, as he clambers down between the deep floor of ice and Satan's shaggy thigh—there "where the thigh curves out to form the haunches"—averts his eyes and language: "Let gross minds conceive my trouble, who cannot see the point I had passed." He means, as we know, earth's center, but he would hardly be Dante to leave it at that. Hell, read the inscription on its gate, was made by "the divine Power, the supreme Wisdom, and the primal Love"—the trinity in action. In Satan's figure, to which we've been led by a parodied Latin hymn, we see these reversed. Power becomes impotence; wisdom, a matter of mechanical gnawing and flapping; love, a congealing wind. As counterpoise to that radiant, all-engendering point in heaven, we may expect something more graphically awful than a fictive locus. "The sacred number *three* is symbolic of the whole male genitalia," writes Freud in the *Introductory Lectures*; it is the source of endless jokes in Greece today. Satan, as an angel, would lack genitals—a touch appropriate to the nullity Dante wishes to convey. For surely this point in hell is where they would have been and are not: a frozen, ungenerative, nonexistent trinity. And it is hardly from squeamishness or to spare his reader that Dante contrives to "miss the point" in hell. He has come a long way since Virgil's own hands prevented a stolen glance at the Medusa. His wiser reticence here implies a risk to the spirit, which might have vanished at a closer look, as into a black hole.

The point—my point and everyone's by now, not these of Dante—is that the *Comedy* throughout sustains the equilibrium we have been told to look for in a haiku by Basho. There is no rift, as in conventional allegory, between action and interpretation, physical and moral, "low" and "high." All is of a piece. It is a mystic's view of the world, if you like. It is also a scientist's. And to have it tally with Einstein? For the year 1300, that's seeing the light in spades.

What diction, then, is even faintly suited to divine grace when it illuminates all things great and small? The answer must lie in the entire range, from the courtly metaphysics of the love poems, on which Dante would draw for his highest flights in paradise, to the broad innuendo of those sonnets to Forese. These also served him, as a farting devil in the Malebolge reminds us. Like the Jongleur de Notre-Dame in the pureness of his heart doing *what he can*, Dante will run through his whole bag of tricks, and the performance will be rewarded by an extraordinary universal Smile.

This wealth of diction and detail gave the *Comedy* its long reputation for a grotesque farrago flawed by "the bad taste of the century." The mature Milton asked *his* Muse to help him soar "with no middle flight"—a costly decision. Whatever its glories, the diction of *Paradise Lost* labors under its moral regalia, its relentless pre-Augustan triumphs over precisely this eclectic middle style which allows Dante his touching, first-person particularity, moles and all. It also suggests why he is continually being rediscovered by poets—now by Hugo, now by Pound—and why translations, especially into verse, keep appearing.

JORGE LUIS BORGES

Nine Dantesque Essays
1945–1951

PROLOGUE

Imagine, in an Oriental library, a panel painted many centuries ago. It may be Arabic, and we are told that all the legends of *The Thousand and one Nights* are represented on its surface; it may be Chinese, and we learn that it illustrates a novel that has hundreds or thousands of characters. In the tumult of its forms, one shape—a tree like an inverted cone; a group of mosques, vermilion in color, against an iron wall—catches our attention, and from there we move on to others. The day declines, the light is wearing thin, and as we go deeper into the carved surface we understand that there is nothing on earth that is not there. What was, is, and shall be, the history of past and future, the things I have had and those I will have, all of it awaits us somewhere in this serene labyrinth.... I have fantasized a magical work, a panel that is also a microcosm: Dante's poem is that panel whose edges enclose the universe. Yet I believe that if we were able to read it in innocence but that happiness is barred to us), its universality would not be the first thing we would notice, and still less its grandiose sublimity. We would, I believe, notice other, less overwhelming and far more delightful characteristics much sooner, perhaps first of all the one singled out by the British Danteans: the varied and felicitous invention of precise traits. In describing a man intertwined with a serpent, it is not enough for Dante to say that the man is being transformed into a serpent and the serpent into a man; he

From *Selected Non-Fictions Jorge Luis Borges* ed. Eliot Weinberger. Trans. by Esther Allen, Suzanne Jill Levine, and Eliot Weinberger (Penguin Putnam, Inc., 1999). © 1999 by Maria Kodama. Reprinted by permission of Penguin Putnam, Inc.

compares this mutual metamorphosis to a flame devouring a page, preceded by a reddish strip where whiteness dies but that is not yet black (*Inferno* XXV, 64). It is not enough for him to say that in the darkness of the seventh circle the damned must squint to see him; he compares them to men gazing at each other beneath a dim moon or to an old tailor threading a needle (*Inferno* XV, 19). It is not enough for him to say that the water in the depths of the universe has frozen; he adds that it looks like glass, not water *Inferno* XXXII, 24) .... Such comparisons were in Macaulay's mind when he declared, in opposition to Cary, that Milton's "vague sublimity" and "magnificent generalities" moved him less than Dante's specifics. Later, Ruskin (*Modern Painters* IV, XIV) also condemned Milton's fog and uncertainty and approved of the strictly accurate topography by which Dante engineered his infernal plane. It is common knowledge that poets proceed by hyperbole: for Petrarch or for Góngora, every woman's hair is gold and all water is crystal. This crude, mechanical alphabet of symbols corrupts the rigor of words and appears to arise from the indifference of an imperfect observation. Dante forbids himself this error; not one word in his book is unjustified.

The precision I have just noted is not a rhetorical artifice but an affirmation of the integrity, the plenitude, with which each incident of the poem has been imagined. The same may be said of the psychological traits which are at once so admirable and so modest. The poem is interwoven with such traits, of which I will cite a few. The souls destined for hell weep and blaspheme against God; then, when they step onto Charon's bark, their fear changes to desire and an intolerable eagerness (*Inferno* III, 124). Dante hears from Virgil's own lips that Virgil will never enter heaven; immediately he calls him "master" and "sir," perhaps to show that this confession does not lessen his affection, perhaps because, knowing Virgil to be lost, he loves him all the more (*Inferno* IV, 39). In the black hurricane of the second circle, Dante wishes to learn the root of Paolo and Francesca's love; Francesca tells him that the two loved each other without knowing it, "*soli eravamo e sanza alcun sospetto*" [we were alone, suspecting nothing], and that their love was revealed to them by a casual reading. Virgil rails against proud spirits who aspire to encompass infinite divinity with mere reason; suddenly he bows his head and is silent, because one of those unfortunates is he (*Purgatorio* III, 34). On the rugged slope of Purgatory, the shade of Sordello the Mantuan inquires of Virgil's shade as to its homeland; Virgil says Mantua. Sordello interrupts and embraces him (*Purgatorio* VI, 58). The novels of our own day follow mental processes with extravagant verbosity; Dante allows them to glimmer in an intention or a gesture.

Paul Claudel has observed that the sights that await us after dying will not, in all likelihood, include the nine circles of Hell, the terraces of Purgatory, or the concentric heavens. Dante would undoubtedly have agreed; he devised his topography of death as an artifice demanded by Scholasticism and by the form of his poem.

Dante's universe is described by Ptolemaic astronomy and Christian theology. Earth is a motionless sphere; in the center of the Boreal hemisphere—the one permitted to mankind—is the Mount of Zion; ninety degrees to the east of that mountain, a river, the Ganges, dies; ninety degrees to the west, a river, the Ebro, is born. The Austral hemisphere consists of water, not land, and is barred to mankind; in the center is a mountain that is the antipode of Zion, the Mount of Purgatory. The two rivers and the two mountains, all equidistant, inscribe a cross on the terrestrial orb. Beneath the Mount of Zion, but considerably wider, an inverted cone—Hell—tapers toward the center of the earth, divided into diminishing circles like the rows of an amphitheater. The circles are nine in number, and their topography is appalling and ruinous; the first five form the Upper Inferno, the last four, the Lower Inferno, a city with red mosques surrounded by walls of iron. Within it are crypts, pits, precipices, swamps, and dunes; at the cone's apex is Lucifer, "the worm that gnaws the world." A crack opened in the rock by the waters of Lethe connects Hell's lowest depths to the base of the Mount of Purgatory, which is an island and has a door. Its slopes are stepped with terraces that signify the mortal sins; at its peak, the Garden of Eden blossoms. Nine concentric spheres spin around the earth; the first seven are the planetary heavens (those of the Moon, Mercury, Venus, the Sun, Mars, Jupiter, and Saturn); the eighth is the Heaven of the Fixed Stars; the ninth, the Crystalline Heaven, also called the Primum Mobile. This is surrounded by the empyrean, where the Rose of the Just opens, immeasurable, around a point, which is God. Predictably, the choirs that make up the Rose are nine in number .... Such are the broad outlines of the general configuration of Dante's world, which is subordinate, as the reader will have observed, to the preeminence of the numbers 1 and 3 and of the circle. The Demiurge of the *Timaeus*, a book mentioned by Dante (*Convivio* III, 5; *Paradiso* IV, 49) considered rotation the most perfect form of movement, and the sphere the most perfect body; this dogma, which Plato's Demiurge shared with

Xenophanes and Parmenides, governs the geography of the three worlds traversed by Dante.

The nine revolving circles and the southern hemisphere made of water with a mountain at its center plainly correspond to an antiquated cosmology; there are those who feel that the same adjective is applicable to the supernatural economy of the poem. The nine circles of Hell (they argue) are no less outdated and indefensible than the nine heavens of Ptolemy, and Purgatory is as unreal as the mountain where Dante places it. A variety of considerations can serve to counter this objection: first, that Dante did not propose to establish the true or realistic topography of the other world. He stated this himself. In his famous epistle to Can Grande, written in Latin, he wrote that the subject of his *Commedia* is, literally, the state of souls after death and, allegorically, man, whose merits and faults make him deserving of divine punishment or reward. Iacopo di Dante, the poet's son, developed this idea further. In the prologue to his commentary, we read that the *Commedia* seeks to paint humanity's three modes of being in allegorical colors, so that in the first part the author considers vice, calling it Hell; in the second, the passage from vice to virtue, calling it Purgatory; in the third, the condition of perfect men, calling it Paradise, "to demonstrate the loftiness of their virtues and their happiness, both of which are necessary to man in order for him to discern the highest good." Other time-honored commentators understood it in the same way; Iacopo della Lana, for example, explains that "the poet, considering human life to be of three conditions, which are the life of the sinful, the life of the penitent and the life of the good, divided his book into three parts, which are Hell, Purgatory and Paradise."

Another trustworthy testimony is that of Francesco da Buti, who annotated the *Commedia* toward the end of the fourteenth century. He makes the words of Dante's letter his own: "The subject of this poem is, literally, the state of souls once separated from their bodies and, morally, the rewards or pains that man attains by the exercise of his free will."

In *Ce que dit la bouche d'ombre*, Hugo writes that in Hell, the shade that appears to Cain in the form of Abel is the same shade Nero recognizes as Agrippina.

Much more serious than the accusation of obsolescence is that of cruelty. Nietzsche, in the *Twilight of the Idols* (1888), gave currency to this notion in the befuddled epigram that defines Dante as "the hyena that *poetizes* on graves"—a definition that is dearly more emphatic than ingenious. It owes its fame, its excessive fame, to the fact that it formulates, with thoughtless violence, a commonplace opinion. The best way to refute that opinion is to investigate the reason for it.

There is a technical explanation for the hardheartedness and cruelty of which Dante has been accused. The pantheistic idea of a God who is also the universe, a god who is every one of his creatures and the destiny of those creatures, may be a heresy and an error if we apply it to reality, but it is indisputable when applied to the poet and his work. The poet is each one of the men in his fictive world, he is every breath and every detail. One of his tasks, and not the easiest of them, is to hide or disguise this omnipresence. The problem was particularly burdensome in Dante's case, for he was forced by the nature of his poem to mete out glory or damnation, but in such a way as to keep his readers from noticing that the Justice handing down these sentences was, in the final analysis, he himself. To achieve this, he included himself as a character in the *Commedia*, and made his own reactions contrast or only rarely coincide—in the case of Filippo Argenti, or in that of Judas—with the divine decisions.

[1945–51/1982] *[EA]*

THE NOBLE CASTLE OF THE FOURTH CANTO

Toward the beginning of the nineteenth century, or the end of the eighteenth, certain adjectives of Saxon or Scottish origin (*eerie*, *uncanny*, *weird*), came into circulation in the English language, serving to define those places or things that vaguely inspire horror. Such adjectives correspond to a romantic concept of landscape. In German, they are perfectly translated by the word *unheimlich*; in Spanish, the best word may be *siniestro*. With this peculiar quality of *uncanniness* in mind, I once wrote, "The Palace of Subterranean Fire that we find in the final pages of William Beckford's *Vathek* (1782) is the first truly atrocious hell in literature. The most famous literary Avernus, the *dolente regno* of the *Commedia*, is not an atrocious place; it is a place where atrocious things happen. The distinction is valid."

Stevenson ("A Chapter on Dreams") relates that in the dreams of his childhood he was pursued by an abominable hue of brown; Chesterton (*The Man Who Was Thursday*) imagines that at the western limits of the world there exists, perhaps, a tree that is more and less than a tree, and at the eastern limits, something else, perhaps a tower, whose very shape is wicked. Poe, in the "MS Found in a Bottle," speaks of a southern sea where the ship itself will grow in bulk like the living body of the seaman; Melville spends many pages of *Moby-Dick* dilucidating the horror of the whale's unendurable whiteness .... I have been lavish with examples; perhaps it would have sufficed to observe that Dante's hell magnifies the idea of a jail;[1] Beckford's, the tunnels of a nightmare.

Several nights ago, on a platform at the Constitución railway station, I suddenly recalled a perfect case of *uncanniness*, of calm, silent horror, at the very entrance to the *Commedia*. An examination of the text confirmed the correctness of this delayed recollection. I am speaking of Canto IV of the *Inferno*, one of the most celebrated.

To one who has reached the final pages of the *Paradiso*, the *Commedia* can be many things, perhaps all things; at the beginning, it is obviously a dream dreamt by Dante, who for his part is no more than the subject of the dream. He tells us he does not know how he found himself in the dark wood, "*tant' era pien di sonno a quel punto*" [I was so full of sleep at the moment]; the *sonno* is a metaphor for the bewilderment of the sinning soul, but it suggests the indefinite onset of the act of dreaming. He then writes that the she-wolf who blocks his path has caused many to live in sorrow; Guido Vitali observes that this information could not have emanated from the mere sight of the beast; Dante knows it as we know things in dreams. A stranger appears in the wood; Dante has only just seen him, but knows that he has long been silent—another bit of oneiric knowledge, justified, Momigliano notes, for poetic, not logical reasons. They embark on their fantastic journey. Entering the first circle of the abyss, Virgil pales; Dante attributes his pallor to fear. Virgil avers that it is pity which moves him, and that he is one of the damned: "*e di questi cotai son io medesmo*" [and I myself am one of these]. To disguise the horror of this affirmation or to express his pity, Dante lavishes him with reverential titles: "*Dimmi, maestro mio, dimmi segnore*" [Tell me, master, tell me, sir]. Sighs, sighs of sadness without torment, make the air shudder; Virgil explains that they are in the hell of those who died before the Faith was established. Four looming shades greet him, neither sorrow nor joy in their faces; they are Homer, Horace, Ovid, and Lucan; in Homer's right hand is a sword, symbol of his sovereignty in the epic. These illustrious phantoms honor Dante as their equal and lead him to their eternal dwelling place, which is a castle encircled seven times by lofty walls (the seven liberal arts or the three intellectual and four moral virtues), and by a stream (earthly goods or eloquence) which they pass over as if it were solid ground. The residents of the castle are persons of great authority; they speak seldom and with gentle voices; their gaze is slow and grave. Within the castle's courtyard is a meadow, mysteriously green; Dante, from on high, sees classical and biblical figures and the occasional Muslim: "*Averois, che'l gran comento feo*" [Averroës, who made the great commentary]. At times, one of them is marked by a trait that makes him memorable—"*Cesare armato, con gli occhi grifagni*" [armed Caesar, with falcon eyes]—or by a solitude that enlarges him: "*e solo, in parte, vidi'l Saladino*" [and by himself apart I saw Saladin]. An arid catalogue of proper names, less stimulating than informative, brings the canto to a close.

A Limbo of the Fathers, also called the Bosom of Abraham (Luke 16:22), and a Limbo for the souls of infants who die without baptism are theological commonplaces; the idea of housing virtuous pagans in this place or places was, according to Francesco Torraca, Dante's own invention. To allay the horror of an adverse era, the poet sought refuge in the great memory of Rome. He wished to honor it in his book, but could not help understanding—the observation is Guido Vitali's—that too great an insistence on the classical world did not accord well with his doctrinal aims. Dante, who could not go against the Faith to save his heroes, envisioned them in a negative Hell, denied the sight and possession of God in heaven, and took pity on their mysterious fate. Years later, imagining the Heaven of Jupiter, he would return to the same problem. Boccaccio says that a long interruption, caused by exile, came between the writing of Canto VII and Canto VIII of the *Inferno*; that fact—suggested or corroborated by the verse "*Io dico, seguitando ch'assai prima*" (I say, continuing, that long before]—may be true, but far more profound is the difference between the canto of the castle and those that follow. In Canto V, Dante made Francesca da Rimini speak immortal words; in the preceding canto, what words might he have given to Aristotle, Heraclitus, or Orpheus if the artifice had occurred to him then? Deliberate or not, his silence deepens the horror and is appropriate to the setting. Benedetto Croce notes: "In the noble castle, among the great and the wise, dry information usurps the place of measured poetry. Feelings of admiration, reverence, and melancholy are stated, not represented" (*La poesia di Dante*, 1920). Commentators have deplored the contrast between the medieval construction of the castle and its classical guests; this fusion or confusion is characteristic of the painting of that era and undoubtedly heightens the oneiric tone of the scene.

In the invention and execution of Canto IV, Dante plotted out a series of circumstances, some of them theological in nature. A devout reader of the *Aeneid*, he imagined the dead in the Elyseum or in a medieval variant of those glad fields; the line "*in loco aperto, luinoso e alto*" [an open place that was luminous and high] recalls the burial mound from which Aeneas saw his Romans, and of the "*largior hic campos aether.*" For pressing reasons of dogma, Dante had to situate his noble castle in Hell. Mario Rossi discovered in this conflict between formal and poetic concerns, between heavenly intuition and frightful damnation, the canto's innermost discord and the root of certain contradictions. In one place it is said that the eternal air shudders with sighs; in another, that there is neither sorrow nor joy in the faces. The poet's visionary faculty had not yet reached its plenitude. To this relative clumsiness we owe the rigidity that gives rise to the singular horror of the castle and its inhabitants, or prisoners. There is something of the oppressive wax museum about this still enclosure: Caesar, armed and idle; Lavinia, eternally seated next to her father. The certainty that tomorrow will be like today, which was like yesterday, which was like every day. A much later passage of the *Purgatorio* adds that the shades of the poets, who are barred from writing, since they are in the *Inferno*, seek to distract their eternity with literary discussions.[2]

The technical reasons—that is, the reasons of a verbal order that make the castle fearsome—can thus be established; but the intimate reasons remain to be determined. A theologian of God would say that the absence of God is sufficient to make the castle terrible. Such a theologian might acknowledge an affinity with the tercet that proclaims the vanity of earthly glories:

> *Non è il mondan romore altro ch'un fiato*
> *di vento, ch'or vien quinci e or vien quindi,*
> *e muta nome perché muta lato.*

[Earthly fame is naught but a breath / of wind which now comes hence and now comes thence, / changing its name because it changes quarter.]

I would propose another reason, one of a personal nature. At this point in the *Commedia*, Homer, Horace, Ovid, and Lucan are projections or figurations of Dante, who knew he was not inferior to these great ones, in deed or potential. They are examples of the type that Dante already was for himself and would foreseeably be for others: the famous poet. They are great, venerated shades who receive Dante into their conclave:

> ch'e si mi fecer della loro schiera
> si ch'io fui sesto tra cotanto senno.

[for they made me one of their company / so that I was sixth amid so much wisdom.]

They are forms of Dante's incipient dream, barely detached from the dreamer. They speak interminably about literary matters (what else can they do?). They have read the *Iliad* or the *Pharsalia* or they are writing the *Commedia*; they are magisterial in the exercise of their art, yet they are in Hell because Beatrice forgets them.

[1951]   [EA]

NOTES

1. "*Carcere cieco*," blind prison, says Virgil of Hell (*Purgatorio* XXII, 103; *Inferno* X, 58–59).

2. In the early cantos of the *Commedia*, Dante was what Gioberti considered him to be: throughout the poem, "a little more than a mere witness to the plot he himself invented" (*Primato morale e civile degli italiani*, 1840).

THE FALSE PROBLEM OF UGOLINO

I have not read all the commentaries on Dante (no one has), but I suspect that in the case of the famous seventy-fifth line of the *Inferno*'s penultimate canto they have created a problem that arises from a confusion of art with reality. In that line, Ugolino of Pisa, after recounting the death of his children in the Gaol of Hunger, says that fasting did more than grief had done ("*Poscia, piú che'l dolor, potè il digiuno*"). I must exempt the earliest commentators—for whom the verse is not problematic—from my reproach; they all take the line to mean that grief could not kill Ugolino, but fasting did. This is also how Geoffrey Chaucer understands it, in the rough outline of the episode he inserted into the Canterbury cycle.

Let us reconsider the scene. At the glacial nadir of the ninth circle, Ugolino infinitely gnaws the nape of Ruggieri degli Ubaldini's neck and wipes his bloodthirsty mouth on that same sinner's hair. He raises his mouth, not his face, from the ferocious repast, and tells how Ruggieri betrayed him and imprisoned him with his children. He saw many moons wax and wane through the cell's narrow window, until he dreamed that Ruggieri, with slavering mastiffs, was hunting a wolf and its cubs on a mountainside. At dawn he heard the pounding of the hammer that was sealing up the entrance to the tower. A day and a night went by, in silence. Ugolino, in his sorrow, bites his hands; his children think he does so out of hunger and offer him their flesh, the flesh he engendered. Between the fifth and sixth day he sees them die, one by one. He loses his sight, and speaks to his dead, and weeps, and gropes for them in the darkness; then fasting did more than grief.

I have said what meaning the first commentators attributed to this final event. Thus, in the fourteenth century, Rimbaldi de Imola: "It amounts to saying that hunger overcame one whom great sorrow could not vanquish and kill." Among the moderns, Francesco Torraca, Guido Vitali, and Tommaso Casini profess the same opinion. Torraca sees stupor and remorse in Ugolino's words; Casini adds, "Modern interpreters have fantasized that Ugolino ended by feeding on the flesh of his children, a conjecture that goes against nature and history," and considers the controversy futile. Benedetto Croce is of the same view, and maintains that of the two interpretations, the most plausible and congruent is the traditional one. Bianchi very reasonably glosses: "Others understand Ugolino to have eaten the flesh of his children, an improbable interpretation, but one that cannot legitimately be discarded." Luigi Pietrobono (to whose point of view I will return) says the verse is deliberately mysterious.

Before taking my own turn in the *inutile controversia*, I wish to dwell for a moment on the children's unanimous offer. They beg their father to take back the flesh he engendered:

> ... *tu ne vestisti*
> *queste misere carni, e tu le spoglia.*
> [... you did clothe us / with this wretched flesh, and do you
> strip us of it.]

I suspect that this utterance must cause a growing discomfort in its admirers. De Sanctis (*Storia della letteratura italiana* IX) ponders the unexpected conjunction of heterogenous images; D'Ovidio concedes that "this gallant and epigrammatic expression of a filial impulse is almost beyond criticism." For my part, I take this to be one of the very few false notes in the *Commedia*. I consider it less worthy of Dante than of Malvezzi's pen or Gracián's veneration. Dante, I tell myself, could not have helped but feel its falseness, which is certainly aggravated by the almost choral way in which all four children simultaneously tender the famished feast. Someone might suggest that what we are faced with here is a lie, made up after the fact by Ugolino to justify (or insinuate) his crime.

The historical question of whether Ugolino della Gherardesca engaged in cannibalism in the early days of February in the year 1289 is obviously insoluble. The aesthetic or literary problem is of a very different order. It may be stated thus: Did Dante want us to believe that Ugolino (the Ugolino of his *Inferno*, not history's Ugolino) ate his children's flesh? I would hazard his response: Dante did not want us to believe it, but he wanted us to suspect it.[1] Uncertainty is part of his design. Ugolino gnaws the base of the archbishop's skull; Ugolino dreams of sharp-fanged dogs ripping the wolves' flanks ("*e con l'agute scane / mi parea lor veder fender li fianchi*"). Driven by grief, Ugolino bites his hands; Ugolino hears his children implausibly offering him their flesh; Ugolino, having delivered the ambiguous line, turns back to gnaw the archbishop's skull. Such acts suggest or symbolize the ghastly deed. They play a dual role: we believe them to be part of the tale, and they are prophecies.

Robert Louis Stevenson ("Some Gentlemen in Fiction") observes that a book's characters are only strings of words; blasphemous as this may sound to us, Achilles and Peer Gynt, Robinson Crusoe and Don Quixote, may be reduced to it. The powerful men who ruled the earth, as well: Alexander is one string of words, Attila another. We should say of Ugolino that he is a verbal texture consisting of about thirty tercets. Should we include the idea of cannibalism in this texture? I repeat that we should suspect it, with uncertainty and dread. To affirm or deny Ugolino's monstrous crime is less tremendous than to have some glimpse of it.

The pronouncement "A book is the words that comprise it" risks seeming an insipid axiom. Nevertheless, we are all inclined to believe that there is a form separable from the content and that ten minutes of conversation with Henry James would reveal to us the "true" plot of *The Turn of the Screw*. I think that the truth is not like that; I think that Dante did not know any more about Ugolino than his tercets relate. Schopenhauer declared that the first volume of his major work consists of a single thought, and that he could find no more concise way of conveying it. Dante, on the contrary, would say that whatever he imagined about Ugolino is present in the debated tercets.

In real time, in history, whenever a man is confronted with several alternatives, he chooses one and eliminates and loses the others. Such is not the case in the ambiguous time of art, which is similar to that of hope and oblivion. In that time, Hamlet is sane and is mad.[2] In the darkness of his Tower of Hunger, Ugolino devours and does not devour the beloved corpses, and this undulating imprecision, this uncertainty, is the strange matter of which he is made. Thus, with two possible deaths, did Dante dream him, and thus will the generations dream him.

[*1948*] [*EA*]

NOTES

1. Luigi Pietrobono observes "that the *digiuno* does not affirm Ugolino's guilt, but allows it to be inferred, without damage to art or to historical rigor. It is enough that we judge it possible" (*Inferno*, 47).

2. Two famous ambiguities may aptly be recalled here, as curiosities. The first, Quevedo's "*sangrienta luna*," the bloody moon that is at once the moon over the battlefields and the moon of the Ottoman flag; the other, the "mortal moon" of Shakespeare's Sonnet 107, which is the moon in the heavens and the Virgin Queen.

THE LAST VOYAGE OF ULYSSES

My aim is to reconsider, in the light of other passages of the *Commedia*, the enigmatic tale that Dante places in the mouth of Ulysses (*Inferno* XXVI, 90–142). In the calamitous depths of the circle where deceivers are punished, Ulysses and Diomedes endlessly burn in a single two-pronged flame. Pressed by Virgil to describe how he met his death, Ulysses relates that after having left Circe, who kept him in Gaeta for more than a year, neither the sweetness of his son, nor the reverence

Laertes inspired in him, nor the love of Penelope could conquer the ardor in his breast to know the world and the defects and virtues of men. With his last ship and the few loyal men left to him, he ventured upon the open seas; they arrived, old men by then, at the narrows where Hercules set his columns. At that outer limit marked by a god to ambition or audacity, he urged his comrades on, to see, since so little life was left to them, the unpeopled world, the untraveled seas of the antipodes. He reminded them of their origin, he reminded them that they were not born to live like brutes, but to seek virtue and knowledge. They sailed toward the sunset, and then to the south, and saw all the stars that the southern hemisphere alone encompasses. For five months their prow cleaved the ocean, and one day they caught sight of a dark mountain on the horizon. It seemed to them higher than any other, and their souls rejoiced. This joy soon turned to grief, for a tempest arose that spun the ship around three times and sank it on the fourth, as pleased Another, and the sea closed over them.

Such is Ulysses' tale. Many commentators, from the anonymous Florentine to Raffaele Andreoli, consider it a digression on the author's part. In their estimation, Ulysses and Diomedes, deceivers, suffer in the pit of the deceivers—"*e dentro dalla lor fiamma si geme / l'agguato del caval*" [and in their flame they groan for the ambush of the horse]—and the journey is no more than an incidental embellishment. Tommaseo, however, cites a passage of the *Civitas Dei*, and could have cited another from Clement of Alexandria, denying that men can reach the lower part of the earth; later, Casini and Pietrobono object to the journey as a sacrilege. Indeed, the mountain glimpsed by the Greek before the abyss entombs him is the holy mountain of Purgatory, forbidden to mortals (*Purgatorio* I, 130–32). Hugo Friedrich acutely observes: "The journey ends in a catastrophe which is not mere human destiny but the word of God" (*Odysseus in der Hölle*, Berlin, 1942).

As he recounts his exploit, Ulysses characterizes it as senseless ("*folle*"); Canto XXVII of the *Paradiso* refers to the "*varco folle d'Ulisse*," to Ulysses' rash or senseless route. The same adjective is applied by Dante in the dark wood to Virgil's tremendous invitation ("*temo che la venuta non sia folle*" [I fear that the coming may be folly]); the repetition is deliberate. When Dante sets foot on the beach Ulysses glimpsed before dying, he says that no one has navigated those waters and been able to return; then he says that Virgil girded him with a bulrush, "*com'Altrui piacque*" [as pleased Another]—the same words spoken by

Ulysses as he declared his tragic end. Carlo Steiner writes: "Was Dante thinking of Ulysses, shipwrecked within sight of this beach? Of course. But Ulysses wished to reach it by relying on his own strength and defying the decreed limits of what mankind can do. Dante, a new Ulysses, will set foot there as a victor, girded with humility and guided not by pride but by reason, illuminated by grace." August Rüegg restates this opinion (*Jenseitsvorstellungen vor Dante* II, 114): "Dante is an adventurer who, like Ulysses, walks along virgin paths, travels across worlds no man has ever glimpsed and aspires to the most difficult and remote goals. But the comparison ends there. Ulysses sets forth on his own account and risks forbidden adventures; Dante allows himself to be guided by higher powers."

Two famous passages justify this distinction. One is where Dante deems himself unworthy to visit the three otherworlds—"*Io non Enëa, io non Paulo sono*" [I am not Aeneas, I am not Paul]—and Virgil announces the mission Beatrice has entrusted to him; the other, where Cacciaguida recommends that the poem be published (*Paradiso* XVII, 100–142). Given this testimony, it would be preposterous to place Dante's peregrination, which leads to the beatific vision and the best book mankind has ever written, on the same level as Ulysses' sacrilegious adventure, which culminates in Hell. The former action seems the reverse of the latter.

This argument, however, contains an error. Ulysses' act is undoubtedly Ulysses' journey, because Ulysses is nothing other than the subject to whom that act is attributed; Dante's act or undertaking is not Dante's journey, but the composition of his book. The fact is obvious, but tends to be forgotten because the *Commedia* is written in the first person, and the man who died has been overshadowed by the immortal protagonist. Dante was a theologian; the writing of the *Commedia* must often have seemed no less laborious and perhaps no less audacious and fatal than the final voyage of Ulysses. He had dared to conjure up arcana that the pen of the Holy Spirit barely indicates; the intention may well have entailed a sin. He had dared to place Beatrice Portinari on the same level as the Virgin and Jesus.[1] He had dared to anticipate the pronouncements of the inscrutable Last Judgment that the blessed do not know; he had judged and condemned the souls of simoniac Popes and had saved that of the Averroëist Siger, who lectured on circular time.[2] So much laborious effort for glory, which is an ephemeral thing!

Non è il mondan romore altro ch'un fiato
di vento, ch'or vien quinci e or vien quindi,
e muta nome perchè muta lato.

[Earthly fame is naught but a breath / of wind which now comes hence and now comes thence, / changing its name because it changes quarter.]

Plausible traces of this discord survive in the text. Carlo Steiner recognized one in the dialogue in which Virgil overcomes Dante's fears and persuades him to undertake his unprecedented journey. Steiner writes, "The debate which by a fiction occurs with Virgil, in reality occurred in Dante's mind, when he had not yet decided on the composition of the poem. It corresponds to the other debate in Canto XVII of the *Paradiso*, which envisages the poem's publication. Having written the work, can he publish it and defy the wrath of his enemies? In both cases, the consciousness of its worth and the high end he had set for himself won out" (*Commedia*, 15). In such passages, then, Dante would have symbolized a mental conflict. I suggest that he also symbolized it, perhaps without wanting to or suspecting he had done so, in the tragic legend of Ulysses, and that its tremendous power is due to that emotional charge. Dante was Ulysses, and in some way he could fear Ulysses' punishment.

A final observation. Devoted to the sea and to Dante, the two literatures written in English have felt the influence of the Dantesque Ulysses. Eliot (and before him Andrew Lang and before him Longfellow) has implied that Tennyson's admirable *Ulysses* proceeds from this glorious archetype. As far as I know, a deeper affinity has not previously been noted: that of the infernal Ulysses with another unfortunate captain: Ahab of *Moby-Dick*. Like his predecessor, he accomplishes his own perdition by means of vigilance and courage; the general story is the same, the grand finale is identical, the last words almost repeat each other. Schopenhauer has written that nothing in our lives is involuntary; both fictions, in the light of this prodigious maxim, describe the process of a secret and intricate suicide.

[1948]   [EA]

Postscript, 1981: It has been said that Dante's Ulysses prefigures the famous explorers who, centuries later, arrived on the coasts of America and India. Centuries before the *Commedia* was written, that human type had already come into being. Erik the Red discovered Greenland around the year 985; his son Leif disembarked in Canada at the beginning of the eleventh century. Dante could not have known this. The things of Scandinavia tend to be secret, as if they were a dream.

NOTES

1. Cf. Giovanni Papini, *Dante vivo* III, 34.
2. Cf. Maurice de Wulf, *Histoire de la philosophie médiévale*.

THE PITYING TORTURER

Dante (as everyone knows) consigns Francesca to the Inferno, and listens with infinite compassion to the tale of her sin. How can this contradiction be lessened, how can it be justified? I see four possible conjectures.

The first is technical. Dante, having determined the general shape of his book, feared that unless it were enlivened by the confessions of lost souls it could degenerate into a worthless catalog of proper names or topographical descriptions. The thought made him place an interesting and not too alien sinner in each of the circles of his Hell. (Lamartine, worn out by these guests, said the *Commedia* was a "*gazette florentine*.") Naturally it was preferable that the confessions be poignant, and they could be poignant without risk, for the author, having imprisoned the narrators in Hell, was safely beyond any suspicion of complicity. This conjecture is perhaps the most plausible (its notion of a poetical orb imposed on an arid theological novel was argued by Croce), but it has a nasty pettiness about it that does not seem to harmonize with our concept of Dante. Moreover, interpretations of a book as infinite as the *Commedia* cannot be so simple.

The second conjecture, following the doctrine of Jung,[1] equates literary and oneiric inventions. Dante, who has become our dream, dreamed Francesca's pain and dreamed his own compassion. Schopenhauer observes that what we see and hear in dreams can astonish us, though ultimately it has its roots in us; Dante, likewise, could feel pity for things he himself dreamed or invented. It could also be said that Francesca is a mere projection of the poet, as, for that matter, is Dante himself, in his role as a traveller through Hell. I suspect, however, that this conjecture is fallacious, for it is one thing to attribute a common origin to books and dreams, and another to tolerate, in books, the disjunction and irresponsibility of dreams.

The third, like the first, is of a technical nature. Over the course of the *Commedia*, Dante had to anticipate the inscrutable decisions of God. By no other light than that of his fallible mind, he attempted to predict certain pronouncements of the Last Judgment. He damned—even if only as a literary fiction—Celestin V and saved Siger de Brabant, who defended the astrological hypothesis of the Eternal Return.

To conceal this operation, he made justice the defining characteristic of God in Hell—"*Giustizia mosse il mio alto fattore*" [justice moved my high maker]—and reserved the attributes of understanding and pity for himself. He placed Francesca among the lost souls, and he felt sorry for Francesca. Benedetto Croce declares, "Dante, as a theologian, as a believer, as an ethical man, condemns sinners; but in sentiment he neither condemns nor absolves" (*La poesia di Dante*, 78).[2]

The fourth conjecture is less precise. A prefatory discussion is required to make it intelligible. Consider these two propositions. One: murderers deserve the death penalty; the other: Rodion Raskolnikov deserves the death penalty. The fact that the propositions are not synonymous is inarguable. Paradoxically, this is not because murderers are concrete and Raskolnikov is abstract or illusory. On the contrary, the concept of murderers betokens a mere generalization; Raskolnikov, for anyone who has read his story, is a real being. In reality there are, strictly speaking, no murderers; there are individuals whom the torpor of our languages includes in that indeterminate ensemble. (Such, in the final analysis, is the nominalist hypothesis of Roscelin and William of Occam.) In other words, anyone who has read Dostoevsky's novel has in some way been Raskolnikov and knows that his "crime" is not free because an inevitable network of circumstances predetermined and dictated it. The man who killed is not a murderer, the man who lied is not an impostor; and this is known (or, rather, felt) by the damned; there is, consequently, no punishment without injustice. The judicial fiction of "the murderer" may well deserve the death penalty, but not the luckless wretch who killed, driven by his own prior history and perhaps—oh Marquis de Laplace!—by the history of the universe. Madame de Staël has compressed these ratiocinations into a famous sentence: "*Tout comprendre c'est tout pardonner*" [To understand all is to forgive all].

Dante tells the story of Francesca's sin with such delicate compassion that all of us feel its inevitability. That is how the poet must have felt it, in defiance of the theologian who argued in the *Purgatorio* (XVI, 70) that if actions depended on the influences of the stars, our free will would be annulled, and to reward good while punishing evil would be an injustice.[3]

Dante understands and does not forgive; this is the insoluble paradox. For my part, I take it that he found a solution beyond logic. He felt (but did not understand) that the acts of men are necessary and that an eternity of heavenly bliss or hellish perdition incurred by those acts is similarly necessary. The Spinozists and the Stoics also promulgated moral laws. Here there is no need to bring up Calvin, whose *decretum Dei absolutum* predestines some for hell and others for heaven. I read in the introductory pages of Sale's *Koran* that one of the Islamic sects also upholds this view.

The fourth conjecture, as is evident, does not disentangle the problem but simply raises it in a vigorous manner. The other conjectures were logical; this last one, which is not, seems to me to be true.

[1948]   [EA]

NOTES

1. Jung's doctrine is somehow prefigured by the classic metaphor of the dream as a theatrical event. Thus Góngora, in the sonnet "*Varia imaginación*" ("*El sueno, autor de representaciones. / En su teatro sobre el viento armado / sombras suele vestir de bulto bello*" [Sleep, author of representations. / Within its theater mounted on the wind / bedecks shadows in lovely forms]); thus Quevedo, in the "*Sueño de la muerte*" ("Once unburdened, the soul became idle, without the labor of the external senses, and in this way the following comedy struck me; and my powers recited it in darkness, with myself as the audience and theater of my fantasies"); thus Joseph Addison, in number 48 of the *Spectator* ("She [the dreaming soul] is herself the theater, the actors, and the beholder"). Centuries before, the pantheist Omar Khayyam composed a strophe translated as follows in McCarthy's literal version: "Now Thou art hidden from all things, now Thou art displayed in all things. It is for Thy own delight that Thou workest these wonders, being at once the sport and the spectator."

2. Andrew Lang writes that Dumas wept when he killed off Porthos. Likewise, we feel Cervantes' emotion at the death of Alonso Quijano, "who, amidst the tears and lamentations of all present, gave up the ghost, or in other words, departed this life."

3. Cf. *De monarchia* I, 14; *Purgatorio* VIII, 73; *Paradiso* V, 19. More eloquent still are the great words of Canto XXXI: "*Tu m'hai di servo tratto a libertate*" [It is you who have drawn me from bondage into liberty] (*Paradiso*, 85).

DANTE AND THE ANGLO-SAXON VISIONARIES

In Canto X of the *Paradiso*, Dante recounts that he ascended to the sphere of the sun and saw around that planet—in the Dantesque economy the sun is a planet—a flaming crown of twelve spirits, even more luminous than the light against which they stood out. The first of them, Thomas Aquinas, announces the names of the others: the seventh is *Beda*, or Bede. Dante's commentators explain that this is the Venerable Bede, deacon of the monastery of Jarrow and author of the *Historia Ecclesiastica Gentis Anglorum*.

Despite the adjective, this, the first history of England, composed in the eighth century, transcends the strictly ecclesiastical. It is the touching, personal work of a man of letters and a scrupulous researcher. Bede had mastered Latin and knew Greek; a line from Virgil could spring spontaneously from his pen. Everything interested him: universal history, the exegesis of Holy Scripture, music, rhetorical figures,[1] spelling, numerical systems, the natural sciences, theology, Latin poetry, and poetry in the vernacular. There is one point, however, on which he deliberately remains silent. In his chronicle of the tenacious missions that finally succeeded in imposing the faith of Jesus on the Germanic kingdoms of England, Bede could have done for Saxon paganism what Snorri Sturluson, five hundred years or so later, would do for Scandinavian paganism. Without betraying his work's pious intent, he could have elucidated or sketched out the mythology of his elders. Predictably, he did not. The reason is obvious: the religion, or mythology, of the Germans was still very near. Bede wanted to forget it; he wanted his England to forget it. We will never know if a twilight awaits the gods who were adored by Hengist, or if, on that tremendous day when the sun and the moon are devoured by wolves, a ship made of the fingernails of the dead will depart from the realms of ice. We will never know if these lost divinities formed a pantheon, or if they were, as Gibbon suspected, the vague superstitions of barbarians. Except for the ritual phrase *"cujus pater Voden"* which figures in all his genealogies of royal lineages—and the case of the cautious king who had one altar for Jesus and another, smaller one for the demons—Bede did little to satisfy the future curiosity of Germanists. He did, however, stray far enough from the straight and narrow path of chronology to record certain otherworldly visions that prefigure the work of Dante.

Let us recall one of them. Fursa, Bede tells us, was an Irish ascetic who had converted many Saxons. In the course of an illness, he was carried off in spirit by angels and rose up to heaven. During his ascension, he saw four fires, not far distant from each other, reddening the black air. The angels explained that these fires would consume the world and that their names were Falsehood, Covetousness, Discord, and Iniquity. The fires extended until they met one another, and drew near him; Fursa was afraid, but the angels told him: "The fire which you did not kindle shall not burn you." Indeed, the angels parted the flames and Fursa reached Paradise, where he saw many admirable things. On his way back to earth, he was threatened a second time by a fire, out of which a demon hurled the incandescent soul of a sinner, which burned his right shoulder and chin. An angel told him: "Now the fire you kindled burns you. For as you accepted the garment of him who was a sinner, so you must partake of his punishment." Fursa bore the stigma of this vision to the day of his death.

Another of these visions is that of a man of Northumbria named Dryhthelm. After an illness that lasted for several days, he died at nightfall, and suddenly came back to life at the break of dawn. His wife was keeping vigil for him; Dryhthelm told her he had indeed been reborn from among the dead and that he now intended to live in a very different way. After praying he divided his estate into three parts, and gave the first to his wife, the second to his sons, and the third to the poor. He bade them all farewell and retired to a monastery, where his rigorous life was testimony to the many dreadful and desirable things that were revealed to him during the night he was dead, which he spoke of thus:

> He that led me had a shining countenance and a bright garment, and we went on silently, as I thought, towards the north-east. We came to a vale of great breadth and depth, but

of infinite length; on the left it appeared full of dreadful flames, the other side was no less horrid for violent hail and cold snow flying in all directions; both places were full of men's souls, which seemed by turns to be tossed from one side to the other, as it were by a violent storm; for when the wretches could no longer endure the excess of heat, they leaped into the cutting cold, and so on infinitely. I began to think that this region of intolerable torments perhaps might be hell. But my guide who went before me answered my thoughts: "You are not yet in Hell."

When he had led me further on, the darkness grew so thick that I could see nothing else but the garment of him that led me. Innumerable globes of black flames rose out of a great pit and fell back again into the same. My leader suddenly vanished and left me alone in the midst of the globes of fire that were full of human souls. An insufferable stench came forth from the pit.

When I had stood there in much dread for a time that seemed endless, I heard a most hideous and wretched lamentation, and at the same time a loud laughing, as of a rude multitude insulting captured enemies. A gang of evil spirits was dragging five howling and lamenting souls of men into the darkness, whilst they themselves laughed and rejoiced. One of these men was shorn like a clergyman; another was a woman. As they went down into the burning pit, I could no longer distinguish between the lamentation of the men and the laughing of the devils, yet I still had a confused sound in my ears. Dark spirits ascended from that flaming abyss beset me on all sides and tormented me with the noisome flame that issued from their mouths and nostrils, yet they durst not touch me. Being thus on all sides enclosed with enemies and darkness, I could not seem to defend myself. Then there appeared behind me, on the way that I came, the brightness of a star shining amidst the darkness; which increased by degrees and came rapidly toward me. All those evil spirits dispersed and fled and I saw that the star was he who had led me before; he turned towards the right and began to lead me towards the southeast, and having soon brought me out of the darkness, conducted me into an atmosphere of clear light. I saw a vast wall before us, the length and height of which, in every direction seemed to be altogether boundless. I began to wonder why we went up to the wall, seeing no door, window, or path through it. Presently, I know not by what means, we were on the top of it, and within it was a vast and delightful field, so full of fragrant flowers that the odor of its delightful sweetness immediately dispelled the stink of the dark furnace. In this field were innumerable assemblies of men in white. As my guide led me through these happy inhabitants, I began to think that this might be the kingdom of heaven, of which I had heard so much, but he answered to my thought, saying "You are not yet in heaven."

Further on I discovered before me a much more beautiful light and therein heard sweet voices of persons singing, and so wonderful a fragrancy proceeded from the place that the other which I had before thought most delicious then seemed to me but very indifferent. When I began to hope we should enter that delightful place, my guide on a sudden stood still; and then turning back, led me back by the way we came.

He then told me that that vale I saw so dreadful for consuming flames and cutting cold is purgatory; the fiery noisome pit is the very mouth of hell; this flowery place is where the souls are received of the just who await the Last Judgment, and the place where I heard the sound of sweet singing, with the fragrant odor and bright light is the kingdom of heaven. "As for you" he added, "who are now to return to your body and live among men again, if you will endeavor to direct your behavior in righteousness, you shall, after death, have a place or residence among these joyful troops of blessed souls; for when I left you for a while, it was to know what your future would be." I much abhorred returning to my body, however I durst not say a word and, on a sudden, I found myself alive among men.

In the story I have just transcribed, my readers will have noted passages that recall—or prefigure—passages in Dante's work. The monk is not burned by the fire he did not light; Beatrice, similarly, is invulnerable to the flames of the Inferno: "*nè fiamma d'esto 'ncendio non m'assale*" [and no flame of this burning assails me].

To the right of the valley that seems without end, torrents of sleet and ice punish the damned; the Epicureans of the third circle endure the same affliction. The man of Northumbria is plunged into despair by the angel's momentary abandonment, as Dante is by Virgil's: "*Virgilio a cui per mia salute die'mi*" [Virgil, to whom I gave myself for my salvation]. Dryhthelm does not know how he was able to rise to the top of the wall; Dante, how he was able to cross the sad Acheron.

Of greater interest than these correspondences, of which there are undoubtedly many more than I have mentioned, are the circumstantial details that Bede weaves into his narrative and that lend a singular verisimilitude to the otherworldly visions. I need only recall the permanence of the burns, the fact that the angel reads the man's silent thought, the fusion of moaning and laughter, the visionary's perplexity before the high wall. It may be that an oral tradition carried these details to the historian's pen; certainly they already contain the union of the personal and the marvelous that is typical of Dante, and that has nothing to do with the customs of allegorical literature.

Did Dante ever read the *Historia Ecclesiastica*? It is highly probable that he did not. In strict logic, the inclusion of the name *Beda* (conveniently disyllabic for the line) in an inventory of theologians proves little. In the Middle Ages, people trusted other people; it was not compulsory to have read the learned Anglo-Saxon's volumes in order to acknowledge his authority, as it was not compulsory to have read the Homeric poems, dosed off in an almost secret language, to know that Homer ("*Mira colui con quella spada in mano*" [Note him there with sword in hand]) could well be chief among Ovid, Lucan, and Horace. Another observation may be made, as well. For us, Bede is a historian of England; to his medieval readers he was a commentator on Scripture, a rhetorician, and a chronologist. There was no reason for a history of the then rather vague entity called England to have had any particular attraction for Dante.

Whether or not Dante knew of the visions recorded by Bede is less important than the fact that Bede considered them worthy of remembrance and included them in his book. A great book like the *Divina commedia* is not the isolated or random caprice of an individual; many men and many generations built toward it. To investigate its precursors is not to subject oneself to a miserable drudgery of legal or detective work; it is to examine the movements, probings, adventures, glimmers, and premonitions of the human spirit.

[1945–51/1957]   [EA]

Note

1. Bede sought the examples he gives of rhetorical figures in the Scriptures. Thus, for synecdoche, where the part stands for the whole, he cited verse 14 of the first chapter of the Gospel According to John, "And the Word was made flesh ...." Strictly speaking, the Word was made not only flesh, but also bone, cartilage, water, and blood.

Purgatorio I, 13

Like all abstract words, the word *metaphor* is a metaphor; in Greek it means "transfer." Metaphors generally consist of two terms, one of which is briefly transformed into the other. Thus, the Saxons called the sea the "whale's path" or the "swan's path." In the first example, the whale's hugeness corresponds to the hugeness of the sea; in the second, the swan's smallness contrasts with the vastness of the sea. We will never know if the inventors of these metaphors were aware of these connotations. Line 60 of Canto I of the *Inferno* reads: "*mi ripigneva là dove'l sol tace*" [she pushed me back to where the sun is silent].

"Where the sun is silent": the auditory verb expresses a visual image, as in the famous hexameter of the *Aeneid*: "*a Tenedo, tacitae per amica silentia lunae*" [from Tenedos, silently in the quiet friendship of the moon].

Beyond discussing the fusion of two terms, my present purpose is to examine three curious lines.

The first is line 13 of Canto I of the *Purgatorio*: "*Dolce color d'oriental zaffiro*" [Sweet hue of oriental sapphire].

Buti explains that the sapphire is a precious stone, of a color between sky blue and azure, most delightful to the eyes, and that the oriental sapphire is a variety found in Media.

In the aforementioned line, Dante suggests the color of the East, the Orient, by a sapphire that includes the Orient in its name. He thus implies a reciprocal play that may well be infinite.[1]

In Byron's *Hebrew Melodies* (1815), I have discovered a similar artifice: "She walks in beauty, like the night."

To accept this line, the reader must imagine a tall, dark woman who walks like the Night, which, in turn, is a tall, dark woman, and so on to infinity.[2]

The third example is from Robert Browning. He includes it in the dedication to his vast dramatic poem, *The Ring and the Book* (1868): "O lyric Love, half angel and half bird…"

The poet says that Elizabeth Barrett, who has died, is half angel and half bird, but an angel is already half bird, and thus a subdivision is proposed that may be interminable.

I do not know whether to include in this casual anthology Milton's controversial line (*Paradise Lost* IV, 323): "the fairest of her daughters, Eve."

To the intellect, the line is absurd, but not, perhaps, to the imagination.

[1945–51/1982]   [EA]

NOTES

1. We read in the initial strophe of Góngora's *Soledades*.

> *Era del año la estación florida*
> *en que el mantido robador de Europa,*
> *media luna las armas de su frente*
> *y el Sol todos los rayos de su pelo*
> *luciente honor del cielo,*
> *en campos de zafiros pasce estrellas.*

[It was in the year's flowery season / that Europa's cloaked abductor / his arms a half-moon on his brow / and all the rays of his hair the Sun / glittering honor of the sky / in fields of sapphires grazes on stars.]

The line from the *Purgatorio* is delicate; that of the *Soledades*, deliberately clamorous.

2. Baudelaire writes, in *"Recueillement"*: "*Entends, ma chère, entends, la douce Nuit qui marche*" [Hear, my darling, hear, the sweet Night who walks]. The silent walking of the night should not be heard.

THE SIMURGH AND THE EAGLE

Literarily speaking, what might be derived from the notion of a being composed of other beings, a bird, say, made up of birds?[1] Thus formulated, the problem appears to allow for merely trivial, if not actively unpleasant, solutions. One might suppose its possibilities to have been exhausted by the multiply feathered, eyed, tongued, and eared *"monstrum horrendum ingens"* [vast, horrible monster] that personifies Fame (or Scandal or Rumor) in Book IV of the *Aeneid*, or that strange king made of men who occupies the frontispiece of the *Leviathan*, armed with sword and staff. Francis Bacon (*Essays*, 1625) praised the first of these images; Chaucer and Shakespeare imitated it; no one, today, considers it any better than the "beast Acheron" who, according to the fifty-odd manuscripts of the *Visio Tundali*, stores sinners in the roundness of its belly, where they are tormented by dogs, bears, lions, wolves, and vipers.

In the abstract, the concept of a being composed of other beings does not appear promising: yet, in incredible fashion, one of the most memorable figures of Western literature, and another of Eastern literature, correspond to it. The purpose of this brief note is to describe these marvelous fictions, one conceived in Italy, the other in Nishapur.

The first is in Canto XVIII of the *Paradiso*. In his journey through the concentric heavens, Dante observes a greater happiness in Beatrice's eyes and greater power in her beauty, and realizes that they have ascended from the ruddy heaven of Mars to the heaven of Jupiter. In the broader arc of this sphere, where the light is white, celestial creatures sing and fly, successively forming the letters of the phrase DILIGITE IUSTITIAM and the shape of an eagle's head, not copied from earthly eagles, of course, but directly manufactured by the Spirit. Then the whole of the eagle shines forth: it is composed of thousands of just kings. An unmistakable symbol of Empire, it speaks with a single voice, and says "I" rather than "we" (*Paradiso* XIX, 11). An ancient problem vexed Dante's conscience: Is it not unjust of God to damn, for lack of faith, a man of exemplary life who was born on the bank of the Indus and could know nothing of Jesus? The Eagle answers with the obscurity appropriate to a divine revelation: it censures such foolhardy questioning, repeats that faith in the Redeemer is indispensable, and suggests that God may have instilled this faith in certain virtuous pagans. It avers that among the blessed are the Emperor Trajan and Ripheus the

Trojan, the former having lived just after and the latter before the Cross.[2] (Though resplendent in the fourteenth century, the Eagle's appearance is less effective in the twentieth, which generally reserves glowing eagles and tall, fiery letters for commercial propaganda. Cf. Chesterton, *What I Saw in America*, 1922.)

That anyone has ever been able to surpass one of the great figures of the *Commedia* seems incredible, and rightly so: nevertheless, the feat has occurred. A century after Dante imagined the emblem of the Eagle, Farid al-Din Attar, a Persian of the Sufi sect, conceived of the strange Simurgh (Thirty Birds), which implicitly encompasses and improves upon it. Farid al-Din Attar was born in Nishapur,[3] land of turquoises and swords. In Persian, Attar means "he who traffics in drugs." In the *Lives of the Poets*, we read that such indeed was his trade. One afternoon, a dervish entered the apothecary's shop, looked over its many jars and pillboxes, and began to weep. Attar, astonished and disturbed, begged him to leave. The dervish answered: "It costs me nothing to go, since I carry nothing with me. As for you, it will cost you greatly to say good-bye to the treasures I see here." Attar's heart went as cold as camphor. The dervish left, but the next morning, Attar abandoned his shop and the labors of this world.

A pilgrim to Mecca, he crossed Egypt, Syria, Turkestan, and the north of India; on his return, he gave himself over to literary composition and the fervent contemplation of God. It is a fact of some renown that he left behind twenty thousand distichs: his works are entitled *The Book of the Nightingale*, *The Book of Adversity*, *The Book of Instruction*, *The Book of Mysteries*, *The Book of Divine Knowledge*, *The Lives of the Saints*, *The King and the Rose*, *A Declaration of Wonders*, and the extraordinary *Conference of the Birds* (*Mantiq al-Tayr*). In the last years of his life, which is said to have reached a span of one hundred and ten years, he renounced all worldly pleasures, including those of versification. He was put to death by the soldiers of Tule, son of Genghis Khan. The vast image I have alluded to is the basis of the *Mantiq al-Tayr*, the plot of which is as follows:

The faraway king of all the birds, the Simurgh, lets fall a magnificent feather in the center of China: tired of their age-old anarchy, the birds resolve to go in search of him. They know that their king's name means thirty birds; they know his palace is located on the Kaf, the circular mountain that surrounds the earth.

They embark upon the nearly infinite adventure. They pass through seven valleys or seas; the name of the penultimate is Vertigo; the last, Annihilation. Many pilgrims give up; others perish. Thirty, purified by their efforts, set foot on the mountain of the Simurgh. At last they gaze upon it: they perceive that they are the Simurgh and that the Simurgh is each one of them and all of them. In the Simurgh are the thirty birds and in each bird is the Simurgh.[4] (Plotinus, too—*The Enneads* V, 8.4—asserts a paradisiacal extension of the principle of identity: "Everywhere in the intelligible heaven is all, and all is all and each all. The sun, there, is all the stars; and every star, again, is all the stars and sun.")

The disparity between the Eagle and the Simurgh is no less obvious than their resemblance. The Eagle is merely implausible; the Simurgh, impossible. The individuals who make up the Eagle are not lost in it (David serves as the pupil of one eye; Trajan, Ezekiel, and Constantine as brows): the birds that gaze upon the Simurgh are at the same time the Simurgh. The Eagle is a transitory symbol, as were the letters before it; those who form its shape with their bodies do not cease to be who they are: the ubiquitous Simurgh is inextricable. Behind the Eagle is the personal God of Israel and Rome; behind the magical Simurgh is pantheism.

A final observation. The imaginative power of the legend of the Simurgh is apparent to all; less pronounced, but no less real, is its rigor and economy. The pilgrims go forth in search of an unknown goal; this goal, which will be revealed only at the end, must arouse wonder and not be or appear to be merely added on. The author finds his way out of this difficulty with classical elegance; adroitly, the searchers are what they seek. In identical fashion, David is the secret protagonist of the story told him by Nathan (II Samuel 12); in identical fashion, De Quincey has proposed that the individual man Oedipus, and not man in general, is the profound solution to the riddle of the Theban Sphinx.

[*1948*]   [*EA*]

NOTES

1. Similarly, in Leibniz' *Monadology* (1714), we read that the universe consists of inferior universes, which in turn contain the universe, and so on *ad infinitum*.

2. Pompeo Venturi disapproves of the election of Ripheus, a personage who until this apotheosis had existed only in a few lines of the *Aeneid* (II, 339, 426). Virgil declares him the most just of the Trojans and adds to the report of his end the resigned ellipsis: *"Dies aliter visum"* [The gods ruled otherwise]. There is not another trace of him in all of literature. Perhaps Dante chose him as a symbol by virtue of his vagueness. Cf. the commentaries of Casini (1921) and Guido Vitali (1943).

3. Katibi, author of the *Confluence of the Two Seas*, declared: "I am of the garden of Nishapur, like Attar, but I am the thorn of Nishapur and he was the rose."

4. Silvina Ocampo (*Espacios métricos*, 12) has put this episode into verse:

> *Era Dios ese pájaro como un enorme espejo:*
> *los contenía a todos; no era un mero reflejo.*
> *En sus plumas hallaron cada uno sus plumas*
> *en los ojos, los ojos con memorias de plumas.*

[Like an enormous mirror this bird was God: / containing them all, and not a mere reflection. / In his feathers each one found his own feathers / in his eyes with memories of feathers.]

THE MEETING IN A DREAM

Having traversed the circles of Hell and the arduous terraces of Purgatory, Dante, now in the earthly Paradise, sees Beatrice at last. Ozanam speculates that this scene (certainly one of the most astonishing that literature has achieved) is the primal nucleus of the *Commedia*. My purpose here is to narrate the scene, summarize the comments of the scholiasts, and make an observation—perhaps a new one—of a psychological nature.

On the morning of the thirteenth day of April of the year 1300, the penultimate day of his journey, Dante, his labors complete, enters the earthly Paradise that crowns the summit of Purgatory. He has seen the temporal fire and the eternal, he has crossed through a wall of flame, his will is free and upright. Virgil has crowned and mitred him over himself (*"per ch'io te sovra te corono e mitrio"*). Along the paths of the ancient garden he reaches a river purer than any other, though the trees allow neither sun nor moon to shine on it. A melody runs through the air, and on the other bank a mysterious procession advances. Twenty-four elders, dressed in white garments, and four animals, each plumed with six wings that are studded with open eyes, go before a triumphal chariot drawn by a griffin; on the right are three women, dancing, one of them so red that in a fire she would barely be visible to us; to the left are four more women, dressed in purple, one of them with three eyes. The coach stops, and a veiled woman appears; her dress is the color of living flame. Not by sight, but by the bewilderment of his spirit and the fear in his blood, Dante understands that she is Beatrice. On the threshold of Glory, he feels the love that so often had pierced him in Florence. Like an abashed child, he seeks Virgil's protection, but Virgil is no longer next to him.

> Ma Virgilia n'avea lasciati scemi
> di sè, Virgilio dolcissimo patre,
> Virgilio a cui per mia salute die' mi.

[But Virgil had left us bereft / of himself, Virgil sweetest father, / Virgil to whom I gave myself for my salvation.]

Beatrice calls out his name imperiously. She tells him he should not be weeping for Virgil's disappearance but for his own sins. She asks him ironically how he has condescended to set foot in a place where man is happy. The air has become populated with angels; Beatrice, implacable, enumerates the errors of Dante's ways to them. She says she searched for him in dreams, but in vain, for he had fallen so low that there was no other means for his salvation except to show him the eternally damned. Dante lowers his eyes, mortified; he stammers and weeps. As the fabulous beings listen, Beatrice forces him to make a public confession .... Such, in my bad prose, is the aching scene of the first meeting with Beatrice in Paradise. It is curious, as Theophil Spoerri observes (*Einführung in die Göttliche Komödie*, Zurich, 1946): "Undoubtedly Dante himself had envisioned this meeting differently. Nothing in the preceding pages indicates that the greatest humiliation of his life awaits him there."

The commentators decipher the scene figure by figure. The four and twenty preliminary elders of Revelations 4:4 are the twenty-four books of the Old Testament, according to St. Jerome's *Prologus Galeatus*. The animals with six wings are the apostles (Tommaseo) or the Gospels (Lombardi). The six wings are the six laws (Pietro di Dante) or the dispersion of holy doctrine in the six directions of space (Francesco da Buti). The chariot is the universal Church; its two wheels are the two Testaments (Buti) or the active and the contemplative life (Benvenuto da Imola) or St. Dominic and St. Francis (*Paradiso* XII, 106–11) or Justice and Pity (Luigi Pietrobono). The griffin—lion and eagle—is Christ, because of the hypostatic union of the Word with human nature; Didron maintains that it is the Pope "who as pontiff or eagle rises to the throne of God to receive his orders and like a lion or king walks the earth with strength and vigor." The women who dance on the right are the theological virtues; those who dance on the left are the cardinal virtues. The woman with three eyes is Prudence, who sees past, present, and future. Beatrice emerges and Virgil disappears because Virgil is reason and Beatrice faith. Also, according to Vitali, because classical culture was replaced by Christian culture.

The interpretations I have mentioned are undoubtedly worthy of consideration. In logical (not poetic) terms they provide an amply rigorous justification of the text's ambiguous features. Carlo Steiner, after supporting certain of them, writes: "A woman with three eyes is a monster, but the Poet does not submit here to the restraints of art, because it matters much more to him to express the moralities he holds dear. Unmistakable proof that in the soul of this greatest of artists, it was not art that occupied the first place, but love of the Good." Less effusively, Vitali corroborates this view: "His zeal for allegorizing drives Dante to inventions of dubious beauty."

Two facts seem to me to be indisputable. Dante wanted the procession to be beautiful ("*Non che Roma di carro così bello, rallegrasse Affricano*" [Not only did Rome with a chariot so splendid never gladden an Africanus]) and the procession is of a convoluted ugliness. A griffin tied to a chariot, animals with wings that are spotted with open eyes, a green woman, another who is crimson, another with three eyes, a man walking in his sleep: such things seem better suited to the circles of the Inferno than to the realms of Glory. Their horror is undiminished even by the fact that some of these figures proceed from the books of the prophets ("*ma leggi Ezechiel che li dipigne*" [but read Ezekiel who depicts them]) and others from the Revelation of St. John. My reproach is not an anachronism; the other paradisiacal scenes exclude any element of the monstrous.[1]

All the commentators have emphasized Beatrice's severity; some, the ugliness of certain emblems. For me, both anomalies derive from a common origin. This is obviously no more than a conjecture, which I will sketch out in a few words.

To fall in love is to create a religion with a fallible god. That Dante professed an idolatrous adoration for Beatrice is a truth that cannot be contradicted; that she once mocked and on another occasion snubbed him are facts registered in the *Vita nuova*. Some would maintain that these facts are the images of others; if so, this would further reinforce our certainty of an unhappy and superstitious love. With Beatrice dead, Beatrice lost forever, Dante, to assuage his sorrow, played with the fiction of meeting her again. It is my belief that he constructed the triple architecture of his poem in order to insert this encounter into it. What then happened is what often happens in dreams: they are stained by sad obstructions. Such was Dante's case. Forever denied Beatrice, he dreamed of Beatrice, but dreamed her as terribly severe, dreamed her as inaccessible, dreamed her in a chariot pulled by a lion that was a bird and that was all bird or all lion while Beatrice's eyes were awaiting him (*Purgatorio* XXXI, 121). Such images can prefigure a nightmare; and it is a nightmare that begins here and will expand in the next canto. Beatrice disappears; an eagle, a she-fox, and a dragon attack the chariot, and its wheels and body grow feathers: the chariot then sprouts seven heads ("*Trasformato così 'l dificio santo / mise fuor teste*" [Thus transformed, the holy structure put forth heads upon its parts]); a giant and a harlot usurp Beatrice's place.[2]

Beatrice existed infinitely for Dante. Dante very little, perhaps not at all, for Beatrice. All of us tend to forget, out of pity, out of veneration, this grievous discord which for Dante was unforgettable. Reading and rereading the vicissitudes of his illusory meeting, I think of the two lovers that Alighieri dreamed in the hurricane of the second circle and who, whether or not he understood or wanted them to be, were obscure emblems of the joy he did not attain. I think of Paolo and Francesca, forever united in their Inferno: "*questi, che mai da me non fia diviso*" [this one, who never shall be parted from me]. With appalling love, with anxiety, with admiration, with envy.

[*1948*]   [*EA*]

NOTES

1. Having written this, I read in the glosses of Francesco Torraca that in a certain Italian bestiary the griffin is a symbol of the devil (*"Per lo Grifone intendo lo nemico"*). I don't know if it is permissible to add that in the Exeter Codex, the panther, a beast with a melodious voice and delicate breath, is a symbol of the Redeemer.

2. It could be objected that such ugliness is the reverse of a preceding "Beauty." Of course, but it is significant .... Allegorically, the eagle's aggression represents the first persecutions; the she-fox, heresy; the dragon, Satan or Mohammed or the Antichrist; the heads, the deadly sins (Benvenuto da Imola) or the sacraments (Buti); the giant, Philippe IV, known as Philippe le Beau, king of France.

BEATRICE'S LAST SMILE

My intention is to comment on the most moving lines literature has achieved. They form part of Canto XXXI of the *Paradiso*, and although they are well known, no one seems to have discerned the weight of sorrow that is in them; no one has fully heard them. True, the tragic substance they contain belongs less to the work than to the author of the work, less to Dante the protagonist than to Dante the author or inventor.

Here is the situation. On the summit of the mountain of Purgatory, Dante loses Virgil. Guided by Beatrice, whose beauty increases with each new circle they reach, he journeys from sphere to concentric sphere until he emerges into the one that encircles all the others, the Primum Mobile. At his feet are the fixed stars; beyond them is the empyrean, no longer the corporeal heaven, but now the eternal heaven, made only of light. They ascend to the empyrean; in this infinite region (as on the canvases of the pre-Raphaelites) distant forms are as sharply distinct as those close by. Dante sees a high river of light, sees bands of angels, sees the manifold rose of paradise formed by the souls of the just, arranged in the shape of an amphitheater. He is suddenly aware that Beatrice has left him. He sees her on high, in one of the circles of the Rose. Like a man who raises his eyes to the thundering heavens from the depths of the sea, he worships and implores her. He gives thanks to her for her beneficent pity and commends his soul to her.

The text then says:

> *Così orai; e quella, sì lontana*
> *come parea, sorrise e riguardommi;*
> *poi si tornò all'etterna fontana.*

[So did I pray; and she, so distant / as she seemed, smiled and looked on me, / then turned again to the eternal fountain.]

How to interpret this? The allegorists tell us: reason (Virgil) is an instrument for attaining faith; faith (Beatrice), an instrument for attaining divinity; both are lost once their end is achieved. This explanation, as the reader will have observed, is as irreproachable as it is frigid; never could these lines have emerged from so paltry a schema.

The commentaries I have examined see in Beatrice's smile no more than a symbol of acquiescence. "Final gaze, final smile, but certain promise," Francesco Torraca notes. "She smiles to tell Dante his prayer has been granted; she looks at him to bear witness to him once again of the love she has for him," Luigi Pietrobono confirms. This assertion (shared by Casini) strikes me as apt, but obviously it only grazes the surface of the scene.

Ozanam (*Dante et la philosophie catholique*, 1895) believes that Beatrice's apotheosis was the primal subject of the *Commedia*; Guido Vitali wonders if Dante, in creating his Paradise, was moved, above all, by the prospect of founding a kingdom for his lady. A famous passage of the *Vita nuova* ("I hope to say of her what has never been said of any woman") justifies or allows for this conjecture. I would go further. I suspect that Dante constructed the best book literature has achieved in order to interpolate into it a few encounters with the irrecuperable Beatrice. More exactly, the circles of damnation and the austral Purgatory and the nine concentric circles and the siren and the griffin and Bertrand de Born are the interpolations; a smile and a voice—that he knows to be lost—are what is fundamental. At the beginning of the *Vita nuova* we read that once, in a letter, he listed sixty women's names in order to slip in among them, in secret, the name of Beatrice. I think he repeats this melancholy game in the *Commedia*.

There is nothing unusual about a wretch who imagines joy; all of us, every day, do the same. Dante does as we do, but something always allows us to catch sight of the horror concealed by these glad fictions. A poem by Chesterton speaks of "nightmares of delight"; this oxymoron more or less defines the tercet of the *Paradiso* I have cited. But in Chesterton's phrase the emphasis is on the word *delight*; in the tercet, on *nightmare*.

Let us reconsider the scene. Dante, with Beatrice at his side, is in the empyrean. Above them, immeasurable, arches the Rose of the just. The Rose is distant, but the forms that people it are sharply defined. This contradiction, though justified by the poet (*Paradiso* XXX, 118), is perhaps the first indication of an inner discord. All at once Beatrice is no longer beside him. An elder has taken her place: "*credea ver Beatrice, e vidi un sene*" [I thought to see Beatrice, and I saw an elder]. Dante is barely able to ask where Beatrice is: "*Ov'è ella?*" he cries. The old man shows him one of the circles of the lofty Rose. There, in an aureole of reflected glory, is Beatrice; Beatrice, whose gaze used to suffuse him with intolerable beatitude; Beatrice, who used to dress in red; Beatrice, whom he thought of so constantly that he was astonished by the idea that some pilgrims he saw one morning in Florence had never heard speak of her; Beatrice, who once refused to greet him; Beatrice, who died at the age of twenty-four; Beatrice de Folco Portinari, who married Bardi. Dante gazes at her on high; the azure firmament is no farther from the lowest depths of the sea than she is from him. Dante prays, as if to God, but also as if to a longed-for woman:

> *O donna in cui la mia speranza vige,*
> *e che soffristi per la mia salute*
> *in inferno lasciar le tue vestige*
> [O lady, in whom my hope is strong, / and who for my
> salvation did endure / to leave in Hell your footprints]

Beatrice looks at him a moment and smiles, then turns away toward the eternal fountain of light.

Francesco De Sanctis (*Storia della letteratura italiana* VII) understands the passage thus: "When Beatrice withdraws, Dante does not utter a single lament: all earthly residue in him has been consumed and destroyed." This is true if we think of the poet's intention; erroneous, if we think of his emotion.

We must keep one incontrovertible fact in mind, a single, humble fact: the scene was *imagined* by Dante. For us, it is very real; for him, it was less so. (The reality, for him, was that first life and then death had taken Beatrice from him.) Forever absent from Beatrice, alone and perhaps humiliated, he imagined the scene in order to imagine he was with her. Unhappily for him, happily for the centuries that would read him, his consciousness that the meeting was imaginary distorted the vision. Hence the appalling circumstances, all the more infernal for taking place in the empyrean: the disappearance of Beatrice, the elder who replaces her, her abrupt elevation to the Rose, the fleetingness of her glance and smile, the eternal turning away of the face.[1] The horror shows through in the words: *come para* refers to *lontana* but contaminates *sorrise*, and therefore Longfellow could translate in his 1867 version:

> Thus I implored; and she, so far away,
> Smiled as it seemed, and looked once more at me …

And *eterna* seems to contaminate *si tornò*.

[1945–51/1982]   [EA]

NOTE

1. The Blessed Damozel painted by Rossetti, who had translated the *Vita nuova*, also unhappy in paradise.

TEODOLINDA BAROLINI

Dante and the Lyric Past

Dante is heir to a complex and lively Italian lyric tradition that had its roots in the Provencal poetry nourished by the rivalling courts of twelfth-century southern France. The conventions of troubadour love poetry—based on the notion of the lover's feudal service to "midons" (Italian "madonna"), his lady, from whom he expects a "guerdon" (Italian "guiderdone"), or reward—were successfully transplanted to the court of Frederick II in Palermo, which became the capital of the first group of Italian vernacular lyric poets, the so-called Sicilian School; the centralized imperial court did not offer a suitable venue for the transplantation of Provence's contentious political poetry, which was left behind. The "leader" (or "caposcuola") of the Sicilian School was Giacomo da Lentini, most likely the inventor of the sonnet (while the Provencal *canso* was the model for the Italian canzone, the sonnet is an Italian, and specifically Sicilian, contribution to the various European lyric "genres"). Giacomo signs himself "the Notary," referring to his position in the imperial government; this is the title Dante uses for him in *Purgatorio* 24, where the poet Bonagiunta is assigned the task of dividing the Italian lyric tradition between the old—represented by Giacomo, Guittone, and Bonagiunta himself—and the new: the avant-garde poets of the "dolce stil novo" or "sweet new style" (*Purgatorio* 24, 57), as Dante retrospectively baptizes the lyric movement that he helped

From *The Cambridge Companion to Dante*, ed. Rachel Jacoff (Cambridge University Press, 1993). © 1993 by Cambridge University Press. Reprinted by permission.

spearhead in his youth. Like Giacomo, the other Sicilian poets were in the main court functionaries: in the *De vulgari eloquentia* Guido delle Colonne is called "Judge of Messina," while Pier della Vigna, whom Dante places among the suicides in Hell, was Frederick's chancellor and private secretary. Their moment in history coincides with Frederick's moment, and the demise of their school essentially coincides with the emperor's death in 1250.

At the heart of troubadour poetry is an unresolved tension between the poet-lover's allegiance to the lady and his allegiance to God; the love-service owed the one inevitably comes into conflict with the love-service owed the other. The conflict is rendered with great clarity in this sonnet by Giacomo da Lentini:

> Io m'aggio posto in core a Dio servire,
> com'io potesse gire in paradiso,
> al santo loco ch'aggio audito dire,
> u' si mantien sollazzo, gioco e riso.

> Sanza mia donna non vi voria gire
> quella c'ha blonda testa e claro viso,
> che sanza lei non poteria gaudere,
> estando da la mia donna diviso.

> Ma no lo dico a tale intendimento,
> perch'io peccato ci volesse fare;
> se non veder lo suo bel portamento

> e lo bel viso e 'l morbido sguardare:
> che lo mi teria in gran consolamento,
> veggendo la mia donna in ghiora stare.

(I have proposed in my heart to serve God, that I might go to paradise, to the holy place of which I have heard said that there are maintained pleasure, play, and laughter. Without my lady I do not wish to go, the one who has a blond head and a clear face, since without her I could not take pleasure, being from my lady divided. But I do not say this with such an intention, that I would want to commit a sin; but rather because I would want to see her beautiful comportment and

her beautiful face and her sweet glance: for it would keep me
in great consolation, to see my lady be in glory.)

This poem both exemplifies the courtly thematic of conflicted
desire, and provides an object lesson in the deployment of the sonnet as
a formal construct The Sicilian sonnet is divided into two parts, set off
from each other by a change in rhyme: the octave rhymes ABABABAB,
and the sextet rhymes CDCDCD. While there are possible variations in
the rhyme scheme of the sextet (it could be CDECDE, for instance),
there is always a switch at this point from the A and B rhymes to a new
set of rhymes; there is always, in other words, a cleavage, created by
rhyme, between the first eight verses and the latter six. It is this cleavage
that "Io m'aggio posto" exploits in such paradigmatic fashion. Giacomo
has perfectly fused form and content: the divisions inherent in the
sonnet form express the divisions experienced by the poet-lover, who is
himself "diviso" in the octave's last word. Moreover, subdivisions within
the octave, divisible into two quatrains, and the sextet, divisible into two
tercets (or, in this case, just as plausibly into three couplets) are also fully
exploited in order to render the two poles of the poet-lover's divided
allegiance.

As compared to the canzone, the lyric genre that allows for
narrative development and forward movement, the sonnet's compact
fourteen-verse form epitomizes a moment, a thought, or a problematic
by approaching it from two dialectical perspectives: in a classic Italian
sonnet, an issue is posed in the octave, and in some way reconsidered or
resolved in the sextet. Looking at Giacomo's poem, we see that the first
quatrain identifies one pole of the poet's desire: he wants to serve God,
to go to paradise. His yearning does not at this stage seem conflicted,
and the entire first quatrain could be placed under the rubric "Dio": "Io
m'aggio posto in core a *Dio* servire." With hindsight we can see that the
potential for conflict is already present in the fourth verse's very
secular—and very courtly—definition of paradise as a place that offers
"sollazzo, gioco e riso": a trio lexically and morally associated not with
the pleasures of paradise, but with the pleasures of the court. But the fact
that there is an alternative pole of desire, an alternative claim on the
lover's fealty, is not made evident until we reach the second quatrain,
which belongs to the "donna" as much as the first quatrain belongs to
"Dio": "Sanza mia *donna* non vi voria gire." Without her he does not
want to go to paradise; the octave has neatly posed the problem with

which the sextet must now deal. And in fact there is a sharp turn toward orthodoxy in the sextet's first couplet, in the initial adversative "Ma," and in the recognition that the lover's stance harbors a potential for sin, "peccato"; but a second adversative, "se non," follows on the heels of the first, negating its negation and reestablishing the poet's will to let the lady dominate. What follows is the listing of those literally "dominant" attributes (as in attributes pertaining to the *domina*) whose absence would render paradise intolerable, a concatenation of three adjective plus noun copulae that gains in momentum and power by being somewhat (in contrast to the otherwise relentlessly clipped syntactical standards of this poem) run on from verse 11 to verse 12: "lo suo bel portamento / e lo bel viso e 'l morbido sguardare." The lady is in the ascendant, and the poem concludes with a poetic resolution that makes the point that there is no ideological resolution to be had. Although the last verse brings together the two terms of the conflict (the lady and "glory," or the lady and paradise), they are yoked in a kind of secularized beatific vision that affirms the poet-lover's commitment not to "Dio," but to the "donna": paradise is only desirable if it affords the opportunity to see "la mia donna in ghiora stare."

From Sicily the lyric moved north to the communes of Tuscany, where it was cultivated by poets like Bonagiunta da Lucca, Dante's purgatorial poetic taxonomist, and Guittone d'Arezzo (d. 1294), the caposcuola of the Tuscan School. Although consistently reviled by Dante for his "municipal" language and excessively ornate and cumbersomely convoluted verse, Guittone set the standard for Tuscan poets to follow, or—in the case of Dante and his fellow practitioners of the "sweet new style"—to refuse to follow. (From a lexical and stylistic perspective, in fact, the new style is best characterized precisely in terms of its rejection of the rhetorical and stylistic norms popularized by Guittone, through a process of winnowing that generated a refined but limited lexical and stylistic range.) A genuinely important poet who rewards study on his own terms, Guittone is responsible for key innovations in the Italian lyric: his *ornatus* derives not just from the Sicilians, but from first-hand appreciation of Provencal language, meter, and rhetoric; as a politically involved citizen of Arezzo, he is the first Italian poet to use the lyric as a forum for political concerns, in the tradition of the Provencal *sirventes*; he experienced a religious conversion (becoming a member of the Frati Godenti c. 1265) that is reflected in his verse, which moves, by way of the conversion canzone

"Ora parra s'eo savero cantare," from love poetry to moral and ethical poetry, and even to religious lauds in honor of St. Francis and St. Dominic. Guittone is thus the first Italian poet to trace in his career a trajectory like that of Dante's (albeit without the epic dimension), and to embrace in his lyrics issues as diverse as the nature of love, in both its secular and divine manifestations, the moral code, with its virtues and vices, and the vicissitudes of Aretine and Florentine politics. Perhaps most significantly, Guittone's thematic innovations are at the service of his bourgeois didacticism, his view of himself as a moral *auctoritas*, a teacher; it is this stance that particularly infuriates his younger rivals, not only Dante but Guido Cavalcanti, who in the sonnet "Da piu a uno face un sollegismo" scorns the notion of Guittone as a source of "insegnamento" ("teaching").

As we can see from the first two stanzas of "Ora parra," Guittone deals with the problem of the lover-poet's dual allegiance by rejecting the troubadour ethos and what he brands carnal love for God and moral virtue:

Ora parra s'eo savero cantare
e s'eo varro quanto valer già soglio,
poi che del tutto Amor fuggh' e disvoglio,
e più che cosa mai forte mi spare:
ch'a om tenuto saggio audo contare
che trovare—non sa ne valer punto
omo d'Amor non punto;
ma' che digiunto—da vertà mi pare,
se lo pensare—a lo parlare—sembra,
ché 'n tutte parte ove distringe Amore
regge follore—in loco di savere:
donque como valere
pò, né piacer—di guisa alcuna fiore,
poi dal Fattor—d'ogni valor—disembra
e al contrar d'ogni mainer' asembra?
Ma chi cantare vole e valer bene,
in suo legno a nochier Diritto pone
e orraro Saver mette al timone,
Dio fa sua stella, e 'n ver Lausor sua spene:
che grande onor ne gran bene no è stato
acquistato—carnal voglia seguendo,

ma promente valendo
e astenendo—*a* vizi' e *a* peccato;
unde 'l sennato—apparecchiato—ognora
de core tutto e di poder dea stare
d'avanzare—lo suo stato ad onore
no schifando labore:
ché già riccor—non dona altrui posare,
ma 'l fa lungiare, —e ben pugnare—onora;
ma tuttavia lo 'ntenda altri a misora.

(Now it will appear if I know how to sing, and if I am worth as much as I was accustomed to be worth, now that I completely flee Love and do nor want it and more than anything else find it very hateful. I have heard it said by a man considered wise that a man not pierced by Love does not know how to write poetry and is worth nothing; but far from the truth this seems to me, if there is concord between thought and word, for in all parts where Love seizes madness is king, in place of wisdom. Therefore how can he have worth or please in any way at all, since from the Maker of all worth he diverges and to the contrary in every way he resembles?

   But he who wants to sing well and be worthy should place Justice in his ship as pilot, and put honored Wisdom at the helm, make God his star and place his hope in true Praise: for neither great honor nor great good have been acquired by following carnal desire, but by living as good men and abstaining from vice and from sin. Therefore the wise man must be prepared at all times with all his heart and power to advance his state to honor, not shunning roil; since indeed riches do not give anyone repose but rather distance it, and good striving brings honor, as long as one pursues it with measure.)

This poem displays essential Guittonian traits. Stylistically, the syntax is anything but clear and limpid, and it is rendered even more convoluted by the complex rhyme scheme with its *rimalmezzo*, or rhyme in the center of the verse (marked by modern editors with hyphens). Thematically, a bourgeois ethic comes into play, as the poet, following his rejection of the troubadour equation between Love and true worth, exhorts us to pursue civic morality and virtuous moderation: although he tells us on the one hand to reject carnal desire (which is what courtly love becomes when stripped of its sustaining ideology), he does not tell us on the other to embrace monastic contemplation. The Guittonian ideal is a life of measured toil and measured gain, leavened by the pursuit of "orrato Saver" and the advancement of one's "stato ad onore": an honored position in the community and a wisdom conceived in terms less metaphysical than practical and ethical.

Our historical assessments of the various alliances that both bound these early Italian poets into schools and polarized them as rivals are not merely the product of an arbitrary need to order the unruly past; in the instance of the emerging Italian lyric, the record shows a keen—and frequently barbed- self-consciousness of such groupings on the part of the poets themselves. Thus, in a sonnet attributed to the Tuscan Chiaro Davanzati ("Di penne di paone"), a fellow poet, perhaps Bonagiunta, is accused of dressing himself in poetic finery stolen from the Sicilian Giacomo da Lentini; the same Bonagiunta will accuse Guido Guinizzelli, the Bolognese poet whom Dante hails as the father of the new style in *Purgatorio* 26, of having altered love poetry for the worse, of having "changed the manner of elegant verses of love" ("Voi, ch'avete mutata la maniera / de li plagenti ditti de l'amore"). Considered a "Siculo-Tuscan" for his use of both Sicilian and Guittonian mannerisms, Bonagiunta is unhappy with the newfangled directions in which Guinizzelli is heading: he does not understand what the "wisdom of Bologna" (a reference to that city's university, noted as a center of philosophical study) has to do with love poetry, and he accuses Guinizzelli of writing pretentious, obscure verse whose philosophical subtleties make it impossible to decode. For modern readers, who find Guittone's rhetorical virtuosity so much more of a barrier than Guinizzelli's modest importation of philosophy into poetry, Bonagiunta's critique may seem misdirected, but his sonnet provides an important contemporary view of the poetic movement that Italian literary historiographers, following Dante, have continued to call the *stil novo*. The exchange between Bonagiunta and the forerunner Guinizzelli will be echoed in later exchanges between conservatives and full-fledged *stilnovisti*; we think of the correspondence between Guido Cavalcanti and Guido Orlandi, for instance, or the parodic indictment of the new style found in the sonnets addressed by Onesto degli Onesti to Dante's friend and poetic comrade Cino da Pistoia.

So, what is this new style that created such consternation among
those contemporary poets who were not its adherents? Initiated by the
older and non-Florentine Guinizzelli (who seems to have died by 1276),
the core practitioners are younger and, with the exception of Cino,
Florentine: Guido Cavalcanti (the traditional birth year of 1259 has
recently been challenged in favor of c. 1250; he died in 1300), Dante
(1265-1321), Cino (c. 1270-1336 or 1337), and the lesser Lapo Gianni,
Gianni Alfani, and Dino Frescobaldi. In characterizing this movement,
Bonagiunta was right to point to the yoking of philosophy—indeed
theology—to Eros. What Bonagiunta could not foresee was the fertility
of a conjoining that would effectively dissolve the impasse that drove
troubadour poetry and give rise to a theologized courtly love,
epitomized by the figure of Dante's Beatrice, the lady who does not
separate the lover from God but leads him to God. But we are getting
ahead of ourselves; Bonagiunta's complaint regarding the theologizing of
love was directed at Guinizzelli, and Guinizzelli s canzone "Al cor gentil
rempaira sempre amore" is an excellent case in point: its fifth stanza
argues that the noble lover should obey his lady in the same way that the
angelic intelligence obeys God, thus implicitly setting up analogies
between the lover and the heavenly intelligence on the one hand, and the
lady and God on the other. As though to acknowledge—and
simultaneously defuse—the radical thrust of his argument, in the *congedo*
Guinizzelli dramatizes an imagined confrontation between himself and
God, by whom he stands accused of having dared to make vain
semblances of the divine, of having presumed to find traces of God's love
in what can only be a "vano amor," a vain earthly love:

> Donna, Deo mi dirà: "Che presomisti?,"
> siando l'alma mia a lui davanti.
>   "Lo ciel passasti e 'nfin a Me venisti,
> e desti in vano amor Me per semblanti;
>   ch'a Me conven le laude
> e a la reina del regname degno,
> per cui cessa onne fraude."
> Dir Li porò: "Tenne d'angel sembianza
> che fosse del Tuo regno;
> non me fu fallo, s'in lei posi amanza."

(Lady, God will say to me: "How did you presume?,", when my soul will be in front of him. "You passed through the heavens and came all the way to me, and you rendered me through the likenesses of vain love; for to me belong the praises and to the queen of the worthy kingdom, through whom all wickedness dies." I will be able to say to him: "She had the semblance of an angel that was of your kingdom; it was no fault in me, if I placed love in her.")

In other words, Guinizzelli has God tell him that he has gone too far. This poet, who has in fact transgressed, pushing to new latitudes the boundaries of the tradition in which he works, finds a supremely witty way of solidifying his gains, of sanctioning his boldness and concretizing what could have seemed merely a whimsical passing conceit: he stages the trial of his presumption ("Che presomisti?" is God's opening argument), registering the indictment but also therefore the self-defense, the justification that he offers before the divine tribunal. It is simply this: the lady possessed the semblance of an angel, of a creature of God's realm; therefore it was not his fault if he loved her. Thus Guinizzelli both acknowledges the dangers of his audacious yoking of the secular with the divine, and brilliantly defends his analogical procedure. If his original "fault" was a too expansive definition of the likenesses through which we can know God ("e desti in vano amor Me per semblanti"), the defense will rest on just such a likeness ("Tenne d'angel sembianza"). Guinizzelli justifies himself with the same analogies which were his sin in the first place, throwing the blame back on the original writer, God, who in his book of the universe made ladies so like angels.

In fact, the *congedo* of "Al cor gentil," with its stated likeness between ladies and angels, backs off somewhat from the canzone's fifth stanza, with its implied likeness between the lady and God himself. The net result of the poem, nonetheless, is to take the possibility of similitude between the lady and the divine much more seriously than it had been taken heretofore, to take her "angelic" qualities out of the realm of amorous hyperbole and into the realm of bona fide theological speculation. With respect to the impasse of troubadour poetry, evoked by Guinizzelli in the "Donna, Deo" conjunction with which the *congedo* begins, we could say that the explicit dramatization of the conflict in "Al cor gentil" goes a long way towards removing it as a problem. In sharp contrast to the troubadours, whose careers are frequently capped by recanting both love and love poetry and retiring to a monastery; in contrast to Giacomo da Lentini, who airs the conflict at its most conflictual in the sonnet "Io m'aggio posto in core a Dio servire"; in contrast to Guittone, who in a bourgeois Italian variation of the troubadour model rejects love but without retiring from secular life; in contrast to all the above, Guinizzelli provides a first step toward the "solution": he begins the process of making the lady more like God so that the two poles of the dilemma are conflated, with the result that the lover does not have to choose between them. Likeness and similitude are Guinizzelli's modes of choice, paving the way for the *Vita nuova* and ultimately the *Commedia*, where similitude will give way to metaphor, as Dante conflates into one the two poles of his desire, making the journey to Beatrice coincide with the journey to God, and collapsing much farther than theology would warrant the distinction between the lady— the luminous and numinous sign of God's presence on earth—and the ultimate being whose significance she figures forth. In the sonnet "Io vogl' del ver la mia donna laudare" ("I want in truth to praise my lady"), Guinizzelli's theologically ennobled lady possesses literally beatific effects: when she passes by, she lowers pride in anyone she greets, makes a believer of anyone who is not, serves as a barometer of moral worth, since she cannot be approached by anyone base, and prevents evil thoughts, since no man can think evilly while he sees her. This poetics of praise, owed to the lady as a literal beatifier, is the Guinizzellian feature that Dante will exploit for his personal *stil novo* as distilled in the *Vita nuova*. In that work Dante builds on and further radicalizes Guinizzelli's "optimistic" notion of love to confect his Beatrice, a lady whose powers to bless (people know her name, "she who beatifies," "she who gives *beatitudine*," without having ever been told) and whose links to the divine are beyond anything yet envisioned within the lyric tradition:

> Ella si va, sentendosi laudare
> benignamente d'umiltà vestuta;
> e par che sia una cosa venuta
> da cielo in terra a miracol mostrare.
>
>   ("Tanto gentile e tanto onesta pare")

(She passes by, hearing herself praised, benignly dressed in humility; and she appears to be a thing come from heaven to earth to show forth a miracle.)

The sacramental and Christological dimensions of the *Vita nuova*'s Beatrice, the fact that she has come from heaven to earth as a manifest miracle, that the portents of her death are the portents of Christ's death, that she *is* the incarnate number nine, take Guinizzelli's solutions an enormous step further along the road from simile ("Tenne d'angel sembianza") to metaphor ("d'umiltà vestuta"), from assimilation to, to appropriation of, the divine.

Along this road that leads in a straight line from the theologized courtly love of the *stil novo* to the incarnational poetics of the *Commedia* there is a magisterial detour, a magnificent dead end (a "disaventura"), and this is the path called Guido Cavalcanti. Guido's poetic "disaventura" can be considered a dead end in two ways: first, with respect to its ideology, which conceives love as a dead-end passion, a sub-rational natural force that leads not to life but to death; second, with respect to its impact on a lyric genealogy that was retroactively pulled into line by the gravitational force of Dante's achievement, which conceives love as a super-rational force that leads not to death but life. So Guido—the "best friend" of the *Vita nuova*, the poet whom both his contemporaries and modern scholarship know as the leader and originator of the stil novo movement, a man whose influence over Dante was not just poetic but personal and biographical—was rendered a detour on the highroad of the lyric by the poet of the *Commedia*, a work that bears the traces of its author's need to define himself as *not* (*inter alias*) Guido Cavalcanti. The negativity that Dante worked so hard to negate is expressed most explicitly and theoretically in the famous canzone "Donna me prega," where Guido assigns love to that faculty of the soul that is "non razionale,—ma che sente" ("not rational, but which feels"), that is, to the seat of the passions, the sensitive soul, with the result that love deprives us of reason and judgment, discerns poorly, and induces vice, so that "Di sua potenza segue spesso morte" ("from its power death often follows"). But one need not look only to the philosophical canzone for Cavalcanti's tragic view of love. Although he sings throughout his verse of a lady who is, like Guinizzelli's lady, supremely endowed with worth and beauty, there is a tragic catch. Yes, she is an "angelicata-criatura" ("angelic creature") and "Oltra natura umana" ("Beyond human nature") in the early *ballata* "Fresca rosa novella," "piena di valore" ("full of worth") in the sonnet "Li mie' foll'occhi,' possessed of "grande valor" ("great worth") in the sonnet "Tu m'hai si piena di dolor la mente," and the litany could go on: Cavalcanti's lady is no less potent than Guinizzelli's. The problem is that she is *too* potent with respect to the lover, whose ability to benefit from her worth has been degraded while she has been enhanced. Thus, in the canzone "Io non pensava che lo cor giammai," Love warns the lover of his impending death, caused by her excessive worth and power: "Tu non camperai, / che troppo e lo valor di costei forte" ("You will not survive, for too great is the worth of that lady"). The poet-lover is dispossessed, stripped of his vitality, integrity, *valore*, his very self: "dirò com'ho perduto ogni valore" ("I will tell how I have lost all worth"), he says in "Poi che di doglia cor. "Because of her *troppo valore*, he will lose *ogni valore*. From the lover's perspective, therefore, her worth is worthless because he has no access to it; it is in fact worse than worthless because it destroys him. As a result, the education of the lover is not an issue for Cavalcanti: in a context where the will is stripped of all potency, its redirection from the carnal to the transcendent becomes a moot point.

The education of the lover is, however, very much the point in the *Vita nuova*: Beatrice is a living lady of this earth, and yet the lover has to be weaned from desiring even as noncarnal an earthly reward as Beatrice's greeting. Unlike Cavalcanti's lady, a carrier of death, Beatrice is truly a "beatrice," a carrier of life, but the "beatitudine" she brings is not of easy access. To find the blessedness/ happiness offered by Beatrice the lover must redefine his very idea of what happiness is. It can have nothing to do with possession (even of the most metaphorical sort), since the possession of any mortal object of desire will necessarily fail him when that object succumbs to its mortality—in short, when it dies. Like Augustine after the death of his friend, he must learn the error of "loving a man that must die as though he were not to die" ("diligendo moriturum ac si non moriturum," *Confessions* 4, 8). Similarly, and painfully, the lover of the *Vita nuova* must learn to locate his happiness in "that which cannot fail me" ("quello che non mi puote venire meno," *Vita nuova* 18, 4), a lesson that constitutes a theologizing of the troubadour *guerdon* along Augustinian lines: because the lady and thus her greeting are mortal and will die, they are objects of desire that—for all their relative perfection—will finally fail him. Therefore the lover must learn to redirect his longing to that which cannot fail him, namely the transcendent part of her with which he can be reunited in God, the part that may indeed serve to lead him to God. Viewed from this perspective, the *Vita nuova* is nothing less than a courtly medieval inflection of the Augustinian paradigm whereby life—new life—is achieved by mastering the lesson of death. The *Vita nuova* teaches us, in the words of Dylan Thomas, that "after the first death there is no other" (from "A Refusal to Mourn the Death, by Fire, of a Child in London"); having encountered the lesson of mortality once, when Beatrice dies, the lover should not need to be taught it again. This is in fact the burden of Beatrice's rebuke to the pilgrim when she meets him in the Earthly Paradise: "e se 'l sommo piacer sì ti fallio / per la mia morte, qual cosa mortale / dovea poi trarre te nel suo disio?" ("and if the supreme pleasure thus failed you, with my death, what mortal thing should then have drawn you into desire?," *Purgatorio* 31, 52—54).

Formally, the *Vita nuova* is a collection of previously written lyrics that, sometime after the death of Beatrice in 1290, most likely in 1292-94, Dante set in a prose frame. The lyrics are chosen with an eye to telling the story of the lover's development, his gradual realization of Beatrice's sacramental significance as a visible sign of invisible grace. They also tell an idealized story of the poet's development, tracing Dante's lyric itinerary from his early Guittonianism (see the double sonnets of chapters 7 and 8), through his Cavalcantianism (see the sonnet that begins with the hapax "Cavalcando" in chapter 9, the *ballata*—Cavalcanti's form par excellence—of chapter 12, and the Cavalcantian torments of the sonnets in chapters 14-16), to the discovery with some help from Guido Guinizzelli—of his own voice in the canzone "Donne ch'avete intelletto d'amore." Prior to the inspired composition of "Donne ch'avete," the poet-lover undergoes the inquisition that induces him to declare that he no longer desires that which is bound to fail him, but instead has centered his desire "in those words that praise my lady" ("In quelle parole che lodano la donna mia," *Vita nuova* 18, 6). The lover's conversion, from one desire (the possession of her greeting) to another (the ability to praise her, to celebrate the miracle of her sacramental existence), is here explicitly stated in poetic terms, is indeed presented as a poet's conversion as well, since his desire for a transcendent Beatrice is formulated as a desire for the words with which to laud her. The *Vita nuova*'s key spiritual lesson is thus aligned with a poetic manifesto for what Dante will call "the style of her praise" ("lo stilo de la sua loda," *Vita nuova* 25, 4). The first poem

we encounter after the conversion of chapter 18 is the canzone "Donne
ch'avete," whose incipit is visited upon the poet in a divine dictation akin
to that described by Dante as the source of his "nove rime" in *Purgatorio*
24; "la mia lingua parlo quasi come per se stessa mossa" ("my tongue
spoke almost as if moved by itself," *Vita nuova* 19, 2) adumbrates the
Purgatorio's famous profession of poetic faith: "I' mi son un che, quando
/ Amor mi spira, noto, e a quel modo / ch'e' ditta dentro vo significando"
("I am one who, when Love in-spires me, takes note, and in that fashion
that Love dictates goes signifying," *Purgatorio* 24, 52–54). "Donne
ch'avete" is canonized in the purgatorial encounter with Bonagiunta as
the prescriptive example of the *stil novo*, the fountainhead and beginning
of the "new rhymes," as though the lyric tradition had no past but
originated with "le nove rime, *cominciando* / 'Donne ch'avete intelletto
d'amore'" ("the new rhymes, *beginning* 'Ladies who have intellect of
love,'" *Purgatorio* 24, 50–51 1; my italics). The authorized version of
Dante's lyric past recounted implicitly by the *Vita nuova* is thus
confirmed by the *Commedia*, where a selective view of the lyric tradition
is put forward through the network of presences and absences,
encounters, statements, and echoes that make up the complicated tissue
of the *Commedia's* vernacular memory.

   In brief, the *Commedia's* version of Dante's lyric past is as follows.
The influence of previous moral/didactic/political poetry is discounted.
Dante denigrates the strongest Italian precursor in this vein, Guittone,
first in the generic distancing of himself from all "old" schools that is put
into the mouth of Bonagiunta in *Purgatorio* 24, then again in *Purgatorio*
26, where—using Guinizzelli as his spokesperson this time—he singles
out the Aretine for attack, ascribing Guittone's erstwhile preeminence to
outmoded tastes. In the same passage, Guinizzelli takes the opportunity
to refer in less than glowing terms to Giraut de Bornelh, the Provencal
poet whose treatment of moral themes Dante had cited with
approbation in the *De vulgari eloquentia*, calling him a poet of "rectitude"
and as such the troubadour equivalent of himself. *Purgatorio* 26 thus
handily liquidates Dante's major vernacular lyric precursors in the
moral/didactic mode. Dante also fails to acknowledge Guittone's
political verse, championing as a political lyricist instead the lesser poet
Sordello in an episode that is not without clear intertextual links to the
displaced Aretine. With regard to the influence of previous vernacular
love poets, the history of Dante's poetic indebtedness is rewritten in a
way that gives disproportionate importance to Guinizzelli: the poetic

"father" of *Purgatorio* 26 absorbs some of the credit due to Guido Cavalcanti as the major stylistic force in the forging of the stil novo. Dante's tribute to the love poet Arnaut Daniel, on the other hand, also in *Purgatorio* 26, is not inconsistent with the influence of the inventor of the sestina on the poet of the *petrose*; but it is worth noting that the exaltation of the Provencal love poet, Arnaut, is at the expense of the Provencal moral poet, Giraut.

Neither the *Vita nuova* nor the *Commedia* intends to tell the full story regarding Dante's lyric past. For that, we have to turn to the lyrics that Dante left as lyrics, that he never pressed into the service of any larger enterprise or ordered among themselves in any way, and that scholars refer to as the Rime. This wonderful collection of eighty-nine poems of definite attribution-sonnets, *ballate*, and canzoni written over a span of approximately twenty-five years (from c. 1283 to c. 1307-08), that is, from Dante's teens to after the *Inferno* was already begun—brings us as close as we can come to the poet's inner workshop, to glimpsing the ways by which Dante became Dante. These poems testify to the paths not taken, and also help us to see more freshly and vividly when, how, and by what slow process of accretion he embarked,on the paths he did take. Moreover, the *Rime* embody the essence of a poetic adventurer; they remind us that Dante's hallmark is his never-ceasing experimentalism, his linguistic and stylistic voracity. Because they vary so greatly among themselves, editors have found it convenient to order them under rough chronological headings, as follows: very early poems written in the Tuscan manner (e.g., the *tenzone* with Dante da Maiano); early poems experimenting in a variety of manners, from the Sicilian (e.g., the canzone "La dispietata mente"), to the playful realism associated with a Folgore da San Gimignano (e.g., the sonnet "Sonar bracchetti"), to the light strains of the Cavalcantian *ballata* (e.g., the *ballata* "Per una ghirlandetta"); poems of the time of the *Vita nuova*, and—whether or not included in the *libello*—written in the style we associate with the *stil novo* (a style that includes, for instance, the love poems dedicated in the *Convivio* to, but in my opinion not originally written for, Lady Philosophy). Through the *stil nova* phase, Dante's poetic agenda is, as Foster and Boyde point out in their edition, one of contraction and refinement; he eliminates both lexically and stylistically to achieve the refined purity of the high *still novo*. The phase of contraction gives way around 1295 to the expansion, both lexical and stylistic, that will characterize the rest of Dante's poetic career and that is pioneered in the following groups of lyrics: the *tenzone* with Forese Donati, written before Forese's death in 1296; the so-called *rime petrose*, or "stony" poems, about a stony, hard, and ice-cold lady, "la pietra," dated internally by "Io son venuto" to December of 1296, moral and doctrinal verse, written most likely between 1295 and 1300, such as the canzone on true nobility, "Le dolci rime," and the canzone on the esteemed courtly quality of *leggiadria*, "Poscia ch'Amor." Finally, there are the great lyrics of exile: the canzone that treats Dante's own exile, "Tre donne"; powerful late moral verse, such as the canzone on avarice, "Doglia mi reca"; and late love poetry, such as the correspondence sonnets exchanged with Cino da Pistoia and the canzone "Amor, da che convien." Although Dante's lyrics are sometimes valued less than the more mono-tonal and unified productions of, say, a Cavalcanti or a Petrarch, it is precisely their infinite variety that is the key to Dante's greatness; they are—with the prose works written during these years— the worthy and necessary prerequisites for a work as nonfinite as the great poem.

The *Rime* contain the traces of Dante's stylistic and ideological experimentation. The *tenzone* of scurrilous sonnets exchanged between Dante and his friend Forese Donati, for instance, was long denied a place among Dante's works because of its base content, considered inappropriate for the refined poet of the *Vita nuova*; and yet, without it, we would be hard put to trace the passage from the tightly circumscribed world of the *Vita nuova* to the all-inclusive cosmos of the *Commedia*. Nor does the *tenzone's* lowly content obscure the archetypal signs of Dante's poetic mastery, evidenced by the compact vigor and concise force of his diction, and the effortless energy with which one insult springs from another. Whereas Forese requires a full sonnet to accuse Dante of being a bounder who lives off the charity of others, Dante characteristically packs an insult into each verse of the opening quatrain of "Bicci novel," which tells Forese that (1) he is a bastard, (2) his mother is dishonored, (3) he is a glutton, and (4) to support his gluttony he is a thief:

> Bicci novel, figliuol di non so cui
> (s'i' non ne domandasse monna Tessa),
> giu per la gola tanta roba hai messa
> ch'a forza ti convien torre l'altrui.

(Young Bicci, son of I don't know who [short of asking my lady Tessa], you've stuffed so much down your gorge that you're driven to take from others.)

(Foster and Boyde, *Dante's Lyric Poetry*, 1, p. 153)

Stylistically, the *Rime* demonstrate continuities converging in the *Commedia*: thus, we can discern in the *tenzone* the seeds of a later vulgar and realistic style associated with *Inferno*. Ideologically, however, the *Rime* offer fascinating examples of discontinuities: thus, the early and generically stilnovist canzoni "E' m'incresce di me" and "Lo doloroso amor" testify to the possibility of an anti-*Vita nuova*, a Cavalcantian *Vita nuova*, whose Beatrice brings not life but death. In "Lo doloroso amor" Dante declares "Per quella moro c'ha nome Beatrice" ("I die because of her whose name is Beatrice"), a scandalous enough assertion for a poet whose career is forged on the notion that "Per quella vivo c'ha nome Beatrice." And in "E' m'incresce di me," the birth of a lady who possesses "homicidal eyes" ("occhi micidiali") is described in language resonant of the *Vita nuova*:

> Lo giorno che costei nel mondo venne,
> secondo che si trova
> nel libro de la mente che vien meno,
> la mia persona pargola sostenne
> una passion nova,
> tal ch'io rimasi di paura pieno

> (The day that she came into the world, according to what is found in the book of my mind that is passing away, my childish body sustained a new emotion, such that I remained full of fear.)

From the perspective of the *Vita nuova* or the *Commedia*, where Cavalcanti is ideologically discounted, what we find here is an impossible hybrid, a fusion of elements that in the more canonical texts are kept separate. There are elements typical of the *Vita nuova*: the treatment of Beatrice's presence, in this case her birth, as a historically and literally miraculous event; the reference to the protagonist's "book of memory," in which the events of his life have been recorded; his juvenile susceptibility to a "passion" defined as "nova," that is, miraculous, unexpected, totally new. But these elements are joined, as they would not be in the *Vita nuova*, to Cavalcantian stylemes: the book of his mind is failing, passing away, while the "passion nova" fills the lover with that most Cavalcantian of emotions, fear.

Dante cannot be pigeonholed; his lyrics are salutary reminders that the dialectical twists of his itinerary cannot be flattened into a straightforward progress. We must remember Dante's sonnet to Cino da Pistoia, written most likely between 1303 and 1306, and thus a decade or so after the spiritualized love of the *Vita nuova*, in which he characterizes love as an overriding force that dominates reason and free will, and admits to having first experienced such love in his ninth year, that is vis-à-vis Beatrice:

> Io sono stato con Amore insieme
> da la circulazione del sol mia nona,
> e so com'egli affrena e come sprona,
> e come sotto lui si ride e geme.
> Chi ragione o virtù contra gli sprieme,
> fa come que' che 'n la tempesta sona.

> (I have been together with Love since my ninth revolution of the sun, and I know how he curbs and how he spurs, and how under him one laughs and groans. He who puts forth reason or virtue against him does as one who makes noise during a tempest.)

"Sotto lui si ride e geme": here the lover is literally "beneath" love's dominion, literally *sommesso*, to use the verb that in *Inferno 5* characterizes the lustful, those who submit reason to desire: "che la ragion sommettono al talento" (*Inferno* 5, 39). As Foster and Boyde comment: "This is the more remarkable in that Dante is now about forty years old and has behind him not only the *Vita nuova* with its story of an entirely sublimated 'heavenly' love, but also the series of canzoni that more or less directly celebrated a love that had its seat in the mind of intellect" (*Dante's Lyric Poetry*, II, p. 323). By the same token, Dante's last canzone is no tribute to sublimation, but "Amor, da che convien pur ch'io mi doglia," a Cavalcantian testament to deadly Eros that has been infused with a decidedly non-Cavalcantian vigor. The poet finds himself in the mountains of the Casentino, in the valley of the Arno where Love's power exerts its greatest strength; here Love works him over (the untranslatable "Cosí m'hai concio"), kneading him, reducing him to a pulp:

> Cosí m'hai concio, Amore, in mezzo l'alpi,
> ne la valle del fiume
> lungo il qual sempre sopra me se' forte:
>   qui vivo e morto, come vuoi, mi palpi,
> merzé del fiero lume
> che sfolgorando fa via a la morte.

(To this state, Love, you have reduced me, among the mountains, in the valley of the river along which you are always strong over me; here, just as you will, you knead me, both alive and dead, thanks to the fierce light that flashing opens the road to death.)

The love-death of "Amor, da che convien," the ineluctable force against which (as explained in "Io sono stato") neither reason nor virtue can prevail, resurfaces in the *Commedia*'s story of Paolo and Francesca, wherein unopposable passion leads to death and damnation. Nor is the condemnation that awaits those unruly lovers without antecedents in the lyrics; roughly contemporaneous with "Io sono stato" and "Amor, da che convien" is the canzone "Doglia mi reca ne lo core ardire," whose indictment of passion ungoverned by virtue and reason inhabits a moral framework that is highly suggestive vis-a-vis the *Commedia*. The breadth and complexity of this canzone can be inferred from its juxtaposition of a courtly discourse with a more strictly ethical and moralizing bent; like Guittone in "Ora parra," but much more systematically, Dante links carnal desire to desire for wealth, thus exploding the courtly ethos that would privilege love over baser desires and illuminating the common ground of all concupiscence. In the second stanza of "Ora parra," cited earlier, Guittone rejects the pursuit of "carnal voglia" ("carnal desire") and recommends a life of abstinence from vice and willingness to toil; then, in an apparent non sequitur, he tells us that "riches do not give anyone repose but rather distance it, and good striving brings honor, as long as one pursues it with measure." Guittone is concerned lest, having exhorted us to reject carnal desire, he may seem—in his pursuit of the good life—to endorse the equally pernicious desire for material gain. The recognition that a repudiation of carnal desire—lust—must not be an endorsement of material desire-avarice—leads to the second stanza's concluding injunction against "riccor" ("riches"), and sets the stage for the fourth stanza's dramatic assertion that it is not we who possess gold but gold that possesses us: "Non manti acquistan l'oro, / ma l'oro loro" ("Not many acquire gold, but gold acquires them"). In other words, Guittone first demystifies courtly love, calling it lust, carnal desire, and then links it to other forms of immoderate and excessive desire, all rooted in cupidity. It is this conflation between lust and greed, love and avarice, that is the key to "Doglia mi reca," a canzone which, although frequently and not incorrectly referred to as Dante's canzone on avarice, and therefore characterized as "stumbling" upon its main theme rather late (Foster and Boyde, *Dante's Lyric Poetry*, II, p. 305), in fact deliberately sets out to graft a discourse on avarice onto its courtly (actually anti-courtly) introduction.

"Doglia mi reca" begins, aggressively enough, by refusing to exculpate women from their share of the moral blame in matters of love; it is their duty to deny their love to men who cannot match in virtue what women offer in beauty. Acknowledging that he will speak "parole quasi contra tutta gente" ("words against almost everyone"), Dante inveighs, in the poem's first stanza, against the "base desire" ("vil vostro disire") that would permit a woman to love an unworthy man. He then announces, in the second stanza, that men have distanced themselves from virtue, and ate therefore not men but evil beasts that resemble men ("omo no, mala bestia ch'om simiglia"); although virtue is the only "possession" worth having, men enslave themselves to vice. The submerged logical link between the phases of this argument is desire: we move from the ladies' "vil disire" for nonvirtuous men in the first stanza, to virtue, the "possession che sempre giova" ("possession that is always beneficial"), that is, the only possession worth desiring, in the second. The point is that men enslave themselves through their desire; by not desiring to possess virtue, the only possession of real worth, and by desiring to possess what is not virtuous, they are doubly enslaved, being, as the third stanza puts it, slaves "not of a lord, but of a base slave": "Servo non di signor, ma di vil servo." Once we grasp the logic that links the two phases of the argument, the courtly to the moral, both viewed as discourses of desire, the fourth stanza's engagement of issues not normally associated with poems addressed to "donne" is less startling:

the man whom the ladies are not supposed to love, the man enslaved to vice, is now compared to the miser in pursuit of wealth. In verses whose irascible energy adumbrates the *Commedia*, Dante depicts the "mad desire" ("folle volere") that induces a man to run after that which can never give him satisfaction:

> Corre l'avaro, ma più fugge pace:
> oh mente cieca, che non pò vedere
> lo suo folle volere
> che 'l numero, ch'ognora a passar bada,
> che 'nfinito vaneggia.
> Ecco giunta colei che ne pareggia:
> dimmi, che hai tu fatto,
> cieco avaro disfatto?
> Rispondimi, se puoi, altro che "Nulla."
> Maladetta tua culla,
> che lusingò cotanti sonni invano;
> maladetto lo tuo perduto pane,
> che non si perde al cane:
> che da sera e da mane
> hai raunato e stretto ad ambo mano
> cio che si tosto si rifa lontano.

(The miser runs, but peace flees faster: oh blind mind, whose mad desire cannot see that the number, which it seeks always to pass, stretches to infinity. Now here is the one who makes us all equal: tell me, what have you done, blind undone miser? Answer me, if you can, other than "Nothing." Cursed be your cradle, which flattered so many dreams in vain; cursed be the bread lost on you, which is not lost on a dog— for evening and morning you have gathered and held with both hands that which so quickly distances itself again.)

The force and vitality of this passage alert us to the fact that Dante has here tapped into a wellspring of his poetic identity. Indeed, the same miser recurs in the *Convivio*, presented in very similar terms: "e in questo errore cade l'avaro maladetto, e non s'accorge che desidera se sempre desiderare, andando dietro al numero impossibile a giugnere" ("and into this error falls the cursed miser, and he does not realize that he desires

himself always to desire, going after the number impossible to reach,"
Convivio III, xv, 9). The miser is a figure through whom Dante explores
the possibility of expanding the problematic of desire from the courtly
and private to the social and public; from this perspective, the miser is an
emblem of the transition from the *Vita nuova* to the *Commedia*. When,
in the final stanza of "Doglia mi reca," Dante readdresses himself to the
ladies, and denounces anyone who allows herself to be loved by such a
man as he has described, he also ties together the poem's threads of
desire into one knot of concupiscence: the depraved call by the name of
"love" what is really mere bestial appetite ("chiamando amore appetito
di fera"); they believe love to be "outside of the garden of reason" ("e
crede amor fuor d'orto di ragione"). Dante has here welded the lover and
the miser, and in so doing he has created a node of enormous
significance for his future, no less than an adumbration of that she-wolf
whose cupidity subtends both the lust of Paolo and Francesca and the
political corruption of Florence. Courtly literature offers us many
examples of lovers whose passion is outside of reason's garden, who are
impelled by the "folle volere" that drives the miser, but courtly literature
never dreams of calling the immoderate lover a miser; nor would the
protagonist of Dante's sonnet "Io sono stato," which boldly proclaims
that reason has no power against love, expect to find himself compared
to an *avaro maladetto*! By making the comparison,. Dante skewers courtly
values, as Guittone had done before him, and then goes further: the
comparison of the lover to the miser lays the foundation for the moral
edifice of the *Commedia*, which is based on the notion of desire or love
as the motive force for *all* our actions. Misdirected or immoderate desire
leads to sin, and is therefore the distant origin for what we witness in
Hell, where the misshapen desire has crystallized into act, as well as the
more proximate origin for what we witness in Purgatory, where the
soul's desires and dispositions are still visible in uncrystallized form.
Love is, in fact, the impulse to which we can reduce all good action and
its contrary: "amore, a cui reduci / ogne buono operare e 'l suo contraro"
(*Purgatorio* 18, 14-15).

I will conclude this discussion of the significance of "Doglia mi
reca" with a formal coda. The *Commedia* is a poem of epic dimension,
epic scale, and yet it is also the most lyric of epics: it is the epic of the "I"
Not only its first-person narrator, but also the lyricized narrative texture
that is ever more present (for, with due respect to Croce, the "lyrical"
canticle is not *Inferno*, but Paradiso) are indices of a lyric past that Dante

chose never to leave behind. One feature of the *Commedia* that points to Dante's vernacular and lyric roots is the canto: why does Dante choose to invent the division into cantos, rather than divide his epic into long books of the sort Virgil uses in the *Aeneid*? Conceptually, I believe that the choice of the canto is connected to Dante's obsession with the new; the division into cantos renders the spiralling rhythm of new dawns and new dusks, the incessant new beginnings and endings that punctuate the line of becoming, the *cammin di nostra vita*. Formally, I believe that the roots of the canto are to be sought in Dante's vernacular apprenticeship. A long canzone is roughly the length of a canto; indeed, at 158 lines "Doglia mi reca" is longer than most cantos. When we think of the *Commedia* as 100 canzoni stitched together, we can better grasp both the later Dante's vertiginous distance from, and remarkable fidelity to, his lyric past.

READING LIST

This century has produced three great editions of Dante's lyrics, each magisterial in its own way. The fruits of Michele Barbi's long philological and historical labors are to be found in two volumes published after his death: M. Barbi and F. Maggini, eds., *Rime della* Vita nuova *e della giovinezza* (Florence: Le Monnier, 1956); M. Barbi and V. Pernicone, eds.,*Rime della maturita e dell'esilio* (Florence: Le Monnier, 1969). Gianfranco Contini's *Rime* of 1946 (Milan: Einaudi, 2nd edn., 1970) remains unsurpassed for the pithiness and elegance of its formulations. The same can be said for Contini's introductions to the various poets represented in his anthology, *Poeti del Duecento*, 2 vols. (Milan-Naples: Ricciardi, 1960). Most useful for its comprehensiveness and for the clarity of the portrait that emerges of the early Italian lyric schools is the edition of Kenelm Foster and Patrick Boyde: *Dante's Lyric Poetry*, 2 vols. (Oxford: Oxford University Press, 1967). On Dante s lyrics in general, see also Patrick Boyde, *Dante's Style in His Lyric Poetry* (Cambridge: Cambridge University Press, 1971); on the *rime petrose* in particular, see the impressively encyclopedic study by Robert M. Durling and Ronald L. Martinez, *Time and the Crystal: Studies in Dante's* Rime petrose (Berkeley: University of California Press, 1990). A thorough review of the cultivators of the early sonnet is provided by Christopher Kleinhenz, *The Early Italian Sonnet: The First Century*

(1220-1321) (Lecce: Milella, 1986). For the *Commedia*'s handling of the vernacular tradition, see Teodolinda Barolini, *Dante's Poets: Textuality and Truth in the* Comedy (Princeton: Princeton University Press, 1984), chapters 1 and 2.

Chronology

1265	Dante is born in Florence.
1266	Guelph victory over the Ghibellines.
1274	Meets Beatrice, the daughter of Folco Portinari.
1277	Engagement to Gemma Donati.
1283	Death of father; Dante is married shortly after to Gemma Donati, with whom he has four children (Jacopo, Pietro, Giovanni, and Antonia).
1289	Takes part in the Battle of Campaldino.
1290	Death of Beatrice.
1292–93	Writes the *Vita Nuova* and begins his study of philosophy.
1295	Joins a guild and enters political life.
1300	Pope Boniface proclaims a Year of Jubilee. In June, Dante becomes one of Florence's seven priors for a two-month term. Easter of 1300 is the date given in *The Divine Comedy* for the beginning of the story's journey.
1301	Sent as ambassador to Pope Boniface. Black Guelphs take Florence in November.
1302	Permanently banished from Florence under penalty of death.
1303–04	*De Vulgari Eloquentia* and the (unfinished) *Convivio* are written sometime during these years.

1306	Interrupts the *Convivio* to write *The Divine Comedy*.
1310	Henry VII of Luxemburg crosses the Alps into Italy. Dante writes epistles supporting Henry's cause. Possible date of the *Monarchia*.
1313	Death of Henry VII.
1314	Completes and publishes the *Inferno*.
1315	Florence offers to repeal Dante's exile if he acknowledges his guilt; he refuses and settles in Verona in the household of Can Grande della Scala.
1319	Moves to Ravenna to the household of Cavalcanti Novella; completes the *Purgatorio*.
1320	Lectures on the *Quaestio de aqua et terra*.
1321	*Divine Comedy* is complete; Dante travels to Venice as an ambassador for Guido Novello; dies on September 13 or 14 from malaria contracted on the journey home.

Works by Dante Alighieri

All dates are necessarily approximate.

Rime, 1283–1308

Detto d'Amore, 1286 (authorship uncertain; widely attributed to Dante)

Fiore, 1286 (authorship also uncertain)

Vita Nuova, 1292–1293

De Vulgari Eloquentia, 1303–1304

Convivio, 1304–1306

Epistolae (letters), 1304–1316

Divina Commedia (*The Divine Comedy*)—*Inferno, Purgatoria, Paradiso*, 1307–1321

Monarchia, 1310–1313

Eclogues, 1319–1321

Quaestio de aqua et terra, 1315

Works about Dante Alighieri

Ascoli, Albert Russell. "*Neminem ante nos*: History and Authority in the *De vulgari eloquentia*." *Annali d'italianistica* 8 1990, 186–231.

———. "The Unfinished Author: Dante's Rhetoric of Authority in *Convivio* and *De vulgari eloquentia*." *The Cambridge Companion to Dante*, ed. Rachel Jacoff. Cambridge: Cambridge University Press, 1993.

Auerbach, Erich. *Dante: Poet of the Secular World*. Chicago: University of Chicago Press, 1961.

———. "Farinata and Cavalcante." *Mimesis*. Princeton: Princeton University Press, 1953.

———. *Literary Language and Its Public in Late Latin Antiquity and in the Middle Ages*. London: Routledge and Kegan Paul, 1965.

———. *Mimesis*. Willard R. Trask, trans. Princeton: Princeton University Press, 1953.

Baranski, Z.G., and P. Boyde, eds. *The* Fiore *in Context: Dante, France, Tuscany*. Notre Dame: University of Notre Dame Press, 1997.

Barolini, Teodolinda. "Dante and the Lyric Past." *The Cambridge Companion to Dante*, ed. Rachel Jacoff. Cambridge: Cambridge University Press, 1993.

———. *Dante's Poets: Textuality and Truth in* The Divine Comedy. Princeton: Princeton University Press, 1984.

———. *The Undivine Comedy: Detheologizing Dante*. Princeton: Princeton University Press, 1992.

Bemrose, Stephen. *A New Life of Dante*. Exeter: University of Exeter Press, 2000.

Bergin, Thomas. *Dante*. New York: Orion, 1965.

Borges, Jorge Luis. "Nine Dantesque Essays." *Selected Non-Fictions*, ed. Eliot Weinberger. New York: Penguin, 1999.

Botterill, Steven. *Dante and the Mystical Tradition*. Cambridge: Cambridge University Press, 1993.

Boyde, Patrick *Perception and Passion in Dante's* Comedy. Cambridge: Cambridge University Press, 1993.

Caesar, Michael, ed. *Dante: The Cultural Heritage*. London and New York: Routledge, 1989.

Curtius, Ernst. *European Literature and the Latin Middle Ages*. Willard R. Trask, trans. Princeton: Princeton University Press, 1990.

D'Atoni, Francesca Guerra. *Dante's Burning Sands: Some New Perspectives*. New York: Peter Lang, 1991.

Durling, Robert M., and Ronald L. Martinez. *Time and the Crystal: Studies in Dante's* Rime Petrose. Berkeley: University of California Press, 1990.

Durling, Robert, ed. and trans. *The Divine Comedy of Dante Alighieri*. New York, Oxford: Oxford University Press, 1996

Ellis, Steve. *Dante and English Poetry: Shelley to T.S. Eliot*. Cambridge: Cambridge University Press, 1983.

Freccero, John. Freccero, John. *Dante: The Poetics of Conversion*. Cambridge: Harvard University Press, 1986.

———. *Dante's Cosmos*. Binghamton: Center for Medieval & Renaissance Studies, State University of New York at Binghamton, 1998.

Harrison, Robert Pogue. *The Body of Beatrice*. Baltimore: Johns Hopkins University Press, 1988.

Higgins, David H. *Dante and the Bible: An Introduction*. Bristol: University of Bristol Press, 1992.

Hollander, R. *Dante's Epistle to Cangrande*. Ann Arbor: University of Michigan Press, 1993

Holloway, Julia Bolton. *Twice-Told Tales: Brunetto Latino and Dante Alighieri*. New York: Peter Lang, 1993.

Jacoff, Rachel, ed. *The Cambridge Companion to Dante*. Cambridge: Cambridge University Press, 1993.

———, and Jeffrey T. Schnapp, eds. *The Poetry of Allusion: Virgil and Ovid in Dante's Comedy*. Stanford: Stanford University Press, 1991.

Kay, Richard. *Dante's Christian Astrology*. Philadelphia, University of Pennsylvania Press, 1994.

Kleiner, John. *Mismapping the Underworld: Daring and Error in Dante's Comedy*. Stanford: Stanford University Press, 1994.

Lansing, Richard, ed. *The Dante Encyclopedia*. New York: Garland, 2000.

Masciandaro, Franco. *Dante as Dramatist*. Philadelphia: University of Pennsylvania Press, 1991.

Mastrobuona, Antonio C. *Dante's Journey of Sanctification*. Washington, DC: Regnery Gateway, 1990.

Mazzocco, Angelo. *Linguistic Theories in Dante and the Humanists*. Leiden: E.J. Brill, 1993.

Mazzotta, Giuseppe. *Dante, Poet of the Desert*. Princeton: Princeton University Press, 1979.

———. *Dante's Vision and the Circle of Knowledge*. Princeton: Princeton University Press, 1993.

———. *Ideas of Order in the Middle Ages*. Binghamton, NY: Center for Medieval and Early Renaissance Studies, 1990.

———, ed. *Critical Essays on Dante*. Boston: G.K. Hall, 1991.

Menocal, María. *The Arabic Role in Medieval Literary Historiography: A Forgotten Heritage*. Philadelphia: University of Pennsylvania Press, 1987.

Menocal, María Rosa. "Synchronicity." *Writing in Dante's Cult of Truth: From Borges to Boccaccio*. Durham: Duke University Press, 1991.

Merrill, James. "Divine Poet." *The Poet's Dante*, eds. Peter S. Hawkins and Rachel Jacoff. New York: Farrar, Straus and Giroux, 2001.

Molho, Anthony, Kurt Raaflaub, and Julia Emlen, eds. *City States in Classical Antiquity and Medieval Italy*. Stuttgart: Verlag, 1991.

Morgan, Alison. *Dante and the Medieval Other World*. Cambridge: Cambridge University Press, 1990.

Pite, Ralph. *The Circle of Our Vision: Dante's Presence in English Romantic Poetry*. Oxford: Clarendon Press, 1994.

Schnapp, Jeffrey T. *The Cambridge Companion to Dante*. Cambridge: Cambridge University Press, 1993.

Shapiro, Marianne. *"De vulgari eloquentia": Dante's Book of Exile*. Lincoln: University of Nebraska Press, 1990.

Singleton, Charles S, ed. *Companion to the Divine comedy / commentary by C.H. Grandgent*. Cambridge: Harvard University Press, 1975.

————, ed. and trans. *The Divine Comedy*. Princeton: Princeton University Press, 1970–1975.

————. "Two Kinds of Allegory." *Dante*. Harold Bloom, ed. New York: Chelsea House Publishers, 1986.

Took, J.F. *Dante, Lyric Poet and Philosopher*. Oxford: Clarendon Press, 1990.

Tusiani, Joseph. *Dante's Lyric Poems*. Brooklyn: Legas, 1992.

Weiss, Julian. *The Poet's Art: Literary Theory in Castile (c. 1400–1460)*. Oxford: Medium Aevum Monographs, 1990.

WEBSITES

Digital Dante (at Columbia University)
dante.ilt.columbia.edu

Dante Online (a web project sponsored by the Societa Dantesca Italiana)
www.danteonline.it

Princeton Dante Project
www.princeton.edu/dante/

Renaissance Editions of Dante
http://www.nd.edu/~italnet/Dante/

Contributors

HAROLD BLOOM is Sterling Professor of the Humanities at Yale University and Henry W. and Albert A. Berg Professor of English at the New York University Graduate School. He is the author of over 20 books, including *Shelley's Mythmaking* (1959), *The Visionary Company* (1961), *Blake's Apocalypse* (1963), *Yeats* (1970), *A Map of Misreading* (1975), *Kabbalah and Criticism* (1975), *Agon: Toward a Theory of Revisionism* (1982), *The American Religion* (1992), *The Western Canon* (1994), and *Omens of Millennium: The Gnosis of Angels, Dreams, and Resurrection* (1996). *The Anxiety of Influence* (1973) sets forth Professor Bloom's provocative theory of the literary relationships between the great writers and their predecessors. His most recent books include *Shakespeare: The Invention of the Human*, a 1998 National Book Award finalist, and *How to Read and Why*, which was published in 2000. In 1999, Professor Bloom received the prestigious American Academy of Arts and Letters Gold Medal for Criticism.

ELLYN SANNA has authored more than 50 books, including adult nonfiction, novels, young adult biographies, and gift books. She also works as a freelance editor and manages an editorial service.

ELIZABETH A. S. BEAUDIN received her Ph.D. from Yale in 1995. She is a medievalist specializing in the treatment of love and lovesickness in early Spanish and Hispano-Arabic texts.

JAMES MERRILL (1926–1995) is a major figure in American letters. Winner of the National Book Award in both fiction and poetry, Merrill received the Pulitzer Prize in 1976 for *Divine Comedies*.

JORGE LUIS BORGES (1899–1986), in addition to playing a major role in Latin-American literature thanks to his fiction and poetry, offered significant and insightful criticism covering a panorama of scholarship, including works on Shakespeare, Joyce, Cervantes, and Whitman. Among his many writings is *1001 Nights*.

TEODOLINDA BAROLINI is Professor of Italian at Columbia University. Among her many scholarly works examining, for example, the works of Dante and Boccaccio, are *Dante's Poets: Textuality and Truth in the* Comedy (1984) and *The Undivine Comedy: Detheologizing Dante* (1992).

INDEX

Centerville Library
Washington-Centerville Public Library
Centerville, Ohio